IMAGES
of America

FLORAL PARK,
NASSAU COUNTY

D1596042

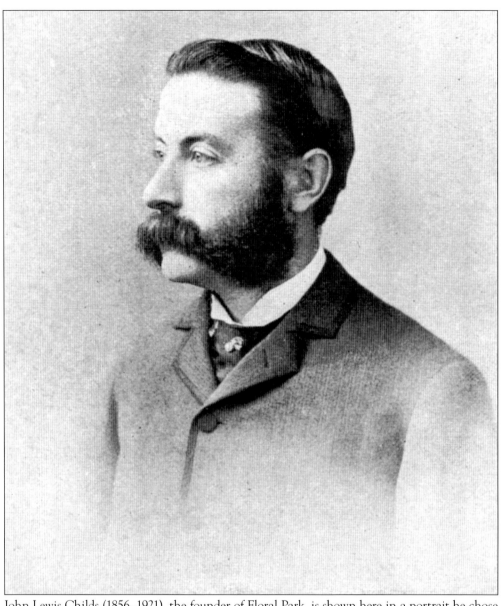

John Lewis Childs (1856–1921), the founder of Floral Park, is shown here in a portrait he chose to include in a booklet he published and printed about the community in 1893. The following year, he was elected as state senator and served for one year. He was generous in his donation of property for the building of churches, funds for the development of higher education, and space on his land for community recreation activities, in addition to being a prosperous businessman. (W. Gosden.)

On the Cover: This pre-1900 image shows the George B. Remsen family in front of their home on the southwest side of Violet Avenue. Pictured from left to right are George B. Remsen Jr., Eugenia Remsen, George B. Remsen Sr., and Mamie Remsen (later to be Mrs. Fred Wrede). Remsen was active in the foundation of Hook and Ladder Company No. 1 of the Floral Park Fire Department in 1893. A street bearing the family name is part of the northwest border of the village. (Floral Park Library.)

IMAGES
of America

FLORAL PARK, NASSAU COUNTY

Walter E. Gosden

ARCADIA
PUBLISHING

Published by Arcadia Publishing
Charleston SC, Chicago IL, Portsmouth NH, San Francisco CA

Printed in the United States of America

Library of Congress Control Number: 2009936563

For all general information contact Arcadia Publishing at:
Telephone 843-853-2070
Fax 843-853-0044
E-mail sales@arcadiapublishing.com
For customer service and orders:
Toll-Free 1-888-313-2665

Visit us on the Internet at www.arcadiapublishing.com

*Dedicated to my grandparents Walter G. and Lillian Gosden
and to my parents, Walter J. and Valerie Gosden,
who encouraged my love of the history of the village
we have resided in for over 85 years.*

CONTENTS

ACKNOWLEDGMENTS

This book would have not been possible without the cooperation and generosity of those that supported my research and dream to honor the village I grew up in. To the mayor and trustees of the Incorporated Village of Floral Park, my thanks for permission to use the images and information in the village and public library archive. The collection of the Floral Park Historical Society was essential to this book, and my sincere gratitude goes to the society's members for their cooperation. Frances Hornberger was librarian for many years and saved much of the material I accessed when researching this book; for this I am most grateful. Jeanne Petta is a great friend who did diligent research into the life of florist Mary Martin and was generous enough to share this information, and her enthusiasm was, and is, an inspiration. Many thanks to the three former village historians: Howard James, Ed Purcell, and Hayden Allen, who preserved important documents, and their interviews with early residents are a great window into the past. Former mayor Ann V. Corbett is an enthusiastic preservationist and had the foresight to have the village purchase a landmark building. This was the most important act of historic preservation in the history of the village. Sincere thanks to Ann, as well as to her husband, Bill, whose friendship and support is most appreciated. Dorethea and Raymond Carson were my primary source of information on vaudeville performers and the business community in Floral Park, and former fire chief William Green contributed information about the fire department, which I appreciated. Edna Krug and John Murphy provided early maps and memories of the village, which were primary sources of information. Many thanks go to James R. Green and Veronica Venturi for technical and computer assistance. Without the patience and support of my wife, Mary, and son, Trevor, I would never have had the time to properly research and write this book. Mary's encouragement and time spent scanning images made this book possible—my sincerest thanks to them.

The images in this book appear courtesy of the Village of Floral Park (VFP), Floral Park Library (FPL), and Floral Park Historical Society (FPHS), unless otherwise noted.

INTRODUCTION

The "Land of Flowers" or "Park of Flowers" has always been used to describe the Village of Floral Park in Nassau County, even before it was a village and Nassau County was yet to be created. The Floral Park Land Company, in an 1894 flyer, stated, "Floral Park, unlike most of the other 'parks,' is exactly what its name indicates, a Park of Flowers. Being the headquarters of the principal seedsman of Long Island, its surrounding land is devoted to the culture of flowers and bulbs, and during the season of growth and bloom its 300 acres of floral beauty furnish an attractive view that is not equaled anywhere."

The community developed because of its close proximity to the two major sources of active commerce at the time: Manhattan and Brooklyn. Convenient transit was another important factor, as the Long Island Railroad's main line goes through the width of the area and the Central Railroad of New York joined it at the center of town. At the time, ferry terminals were not too far distant either.

The western edge of the Hempstead Plains is where Floral Park is located, and the ground proved fertile for farmers to cultivate crops, which would then be harvested and brought to the market to sell. The Wicks were farmers and owned much of the land in the area. They sold directly to buyers, dealers, and pushcart peddlers, and would stay in Brooklyn overnight and rest the horses before returning to Floral Park.

Produce was not the only thing grown locally; flowers were cultivated as well. The earliest grower of flowers was Louis Siebrecht, whose cut-flower business supplied customers in New York City on a daily basis for decades. His acreage was located adjacent to the railroad tracks, which enabled easy loading of his flowers. Charles Linneaus Allen was based in Brooklyn at Columbia and Doughty Streets, and later at Fulton Street. He moved to the corner of Little Neck Road and Jericho Road in 1873, and it was in 1874 that John Lewis Childs of Buckfield, Maine, wrote to Charles Allen seeking employment. Childs arrived in East Hinsdale, Queens County, as it was then known, and that would be the turning point in the development of the area.

There were a number of florists and seed and bulb growers in Floral Park. C. Vernon and Charles Stryker had greenhouses on North Tyson Avenue, Charles H. Allen had greenhouses on Verbena Avenue, Joel Hayden had a cut-flower business, and John Roscoe Fuller, who was Childs's brother-in-law, had an active mail-order business as well. John Lewis Childs developed the cultivation of bulbs, seeds, and plants into a major business and gave the name Floral Park to the area he began to call home.

In order to sell his packets of seeds, bulbs, and plants, Childs immediately realized mail-order sales would be his primary source of revenue. A post office was established at Floral, Queens County, on May 27, 1884, with J. L. Childs as postmaster. Two months later the name was changed to East Hinsdale. The final name change came in October 1891, when East Hinsdale was discontinued, and mail was then sent to or postmarked Floral Park.

Although numerous seedsmen and florists of Floral Park have been mentioned over the years, one escaped any credit at all for more than a century. The existence of a single woman who had a mail-order seed business on Jericho Road for over 25 years never saw any mention. Mary E. Martin issued her first mail-order seed and bulb catalog as early as 1896 and continued to issue catalogs up until at least World War I. Her business was located on Jericho Road, extending north along Hawthorne Avenue. If women of this era worked at all, it was as midwives, domestic help, or in their husbands' stores. Here was a single woman who owned her own business, with considerable competition from local male counterparts. Her catalogs noted she personally handled all orders and did not have family members manage the business for her. This was a thinly veiled comment about John Lewis Childs, who had his wife's brother, Arthur Goldsmith, as manager of his large enterprise.

The late 1880s and 1890s was a period of rapid growth and change in Floral Park. Large commercial buildings started to appear on the landscape, as commerce and population increased. A huge, brick, fireproof seed house was built by Childs on Tulip Avenue just north of the railroad in 1888—the same year his son, Vernon, was born. Childs also started a newspaper titled the *Island* in April 1891. Six months earlier, the cornerstone for the first church to be built in Floral Park was laid a block south of Tulip Avenue, the former Light Horse Road. John Lewis Childs donated the land, and the Methodist Episcopal church was dedicated on June 21, 1891.

Childs's workforce came from people living in the surrounding communities of New Hyde Park, Elmont, and Franklin Square, as well as from Floral Park. His philanthropy was in evidence early on. Many employees from Franklin Square were of German decent, and when seeking to purchase a large plot of land Childs owned in their hamlet, Childs did not sell them the land but instead donated it. Thus the St. Catherine of Sienna Roman Catholic Church could be built in 1908.

Childs continued to build more structures. The Mayflower Press, which was equipped to print the many catalogs, seed packets, and flyers, was a masonry building constructed on Tyson Avenue next to the railroad. The Park House Hotel was a large multistory, wood structure built on Tulip and Violet Avenues. Both were constructed in 1892, during the same era when Childs also built the Tuxedo Apartment House, a six-family dwelling, on Iris Avenue. The apartment house and hotel provided a home for some of Childs's employees at a reasonable rent.

George Tyson was a major property owner, and maps of this period indicate he owned land on the north side of Jericho Turnpike, from Emerson Avenue east to Tyson Avenue. He also built a large office and apartment building in 1893 on the road parallel to the railroad tracks, now known as Tyson Avenue. The wood structure burned down within a few months, and by 1894, a masonry building of the exact same size and style was constructed and deemed the Tyson Building.

The Homestead Hotel, on Jericho Turnpike at the eastern edge of town, was the oldest hotel in the village, and the Wicks family was its longtime owners. To deter early automobiles from speeding along near this spot, a heavy rope would be run across the road to act as a barrier and slow them down.

When ships wrecked on the south shore of Long Island their cargo was salvaged, and on several occasions, kerosene in 5-gallon drums was peddled in Floral Park. Coal and wood were sources of heat for homes, and ash remains were emptied out at the curb at the edge of the street. Water mains were installed primarily by Italian immigrants, who dug the ditches to lay the wood pipes in the streets by hand. George Bickelhaupt had a horse-drawn wagon and collected the trash once a week. It was often dumped in the low wooded area at the south part of town or between the railroad tracks where they merged near an old coal yard. The garbage would attract vermin, and a local ritual was for boys with .22-caliber rifles to shoot at the rats to dispose of them.

For recreation, adult men played poker at people's houses. Children had bicycles and homemade scooters to use, along with ice and roller skates. Jump rope, tag, and marbles were popular games as well. The weekly Sunday afternoon baseball games, held on fields owned by John Lewis Childs, drew many spectators, and when movies made their debut, they were shown at Childs Hall, where dance classes were also held.

In 1894, the Floral Park School was built on South Tyson Avenue. The former schoolhouse was located more than 1 mile west on Jericho Road, where Hook Creek Boulevard joined in.

Former village president George Downing recalled that his mother taught school in that one-room schoolhouse, and she started working there on October 21, 1861. The new school on South Tyson Avenue was built on property purchased from a Mrs. Spooner for $2,000. When children graduated from the Floral Park School, they went to Jamaica High School, taking the trolley there and back each day. Later students also attended Hempstead High School. The coal-burning steam trains just south of the Floral Park School threw off so much ash and soot that it took much effort to keep windowsills and toys in the classroom clean when the windows were left open for ventilation in warm weather, recalled Malvina Wyntzen in a 1983 interview.

Floral Park had been part of Queens County until 1899, when 70 percent of the eastern section of Queens was divided off to create Nassau County. In 1894, John Lewis Childs was elected state senator from Queens County. He spent considerable time at the state capital in Albany but remained state senator for only one year.

Mary Caroline Goldsmith Childs was active in community events in Floral Park and, with several friends, organized the Floral Park Women's Club in 1898. She served as its first president. It became an active organization and has continued its success today.

As the 20th century approached, more buildings were constructed along Jericho Turnpike. Real estate developers placed advertisements in Brooklyn newspapers and had excursion trains transfer prospective buyers to the area where land was being divided into building lots. Childs started to divide and sell off his property as well. He was a great naturalist and close friend of John Burroughs, who visited Childs at his Floral Park home.

In 1902, John Lewis Childs started to collect birds and bird eggs for his private museum collection, and an article in the *Brooklyn Daily Eagle* on January 23, 1910, noted, "He is a very careful collector and does not believe in the general slaughter of birds just for the sake of killing them." The newspaper called Childs "the Bird man of Floral Park."

After 1900, many things took place that affected the growth of Floral Park or came about due to the growth that had already taken place. The first firehouse was built on Violet Avenue, just behind the Park House Hotel. There was a meeting hall on the second floor, and numerous groups would use this new facility. In 1902, the first Catholic church was established in Floral Park on Jericho Turnpike at its eastern edge. St. Hedwig's church served the large population of Polish people who had settled in that area, as well as those in neighboring New Hyde Park, who worked on the farms in the area and for John Lewis Childs. Masses were given in Polish, and eventually a parochial school was established and built on property at the back of the church.

The first Vanderbilt Cup race for motorcars ran through Floral Park in 1904, and in 1905, the Westchester Racing Association opened Belmont Park Race Track on the western border of Floral Park in the hamlet of Elmont. The huge horse racing track attracted people to the area, many traveling through Floral Park and stopping to patronize local businesses. The establishment of the Belmont Stakes annual horse race became the third and final leg of the famous Triple Crown of horse racing in the United States.

The annual Fireman's Day event was of utmost importance to the entire community, who decorated their houses and stores, and hung candle-lit lanterns on their porches in honor of the occasion. Numerous activities took place, including awards for the best decorated house and business. A parade was held and ended at the firehouse on Violet Avenue, where bands would play music and festivities would continue.

The Wright family general store was in existence since 1892, and Edward Baylor ran a butcher shop there. Leo Levy moved to this building in 1904, and the Levy family remained at that location for the next half century.

Additional business people in town were William Hatter, who had a grocery store on Tyson Avenue opposite Richter's Hotel. Joseph Rose purchased property in Floral Park and had a farm on Carnation Avenue adjacent to the railroad tracks. He also owned a hotel and tavern next to the tracks. This property had been owned by Louis Siebrecht and then by John Louis Childs. In 1911, Rose built the first modern block of attached stores with apartments on the south side of Jericho Turnpike, east of Tyson Avenue. At the western edge of the village, Marshall Frost had a grocery store on Jericho Turnpike at the corner of Remsen Lane. It was an era of a proliferation of small, local butcher shops and grocery stores to serve the immediate area, as food would be purchased often by families due to lack of refrigerators. The O'Shansky family had a confectionery store on the north side of Jericho Turnpike and later built a store on Tulip Avenue, where they remained for decades.

The village was incorporated on October 15, 1908, and continued to grow. The House and Home Company built homes along Elizabeth Street. In 1983, Sara Levy, whose family owned the local grocery store, recalled that the greatest concern during a snowstorm was the fear of fire, due to the fact the fire wagon would not be able to get through. Gas and electric service was not prevalent until after World War I. The large annual parties the Childs family held for local children were discontinued around 1918 due to the polio epidemic, a time when large gatherings of children were avoided.

The first village president was John Lewis Childs, and the head of the village continued to be addressed by this title until July 1927, when the title was changed to mayor. The main business area on Tulip Avenue saw dramatic change in 1928, when the wood structures were torn down and modern stores with apartments were built on both sides of the street, from the railroad tracks to Iris Avenue. The eastern edge of the village, known as the Hillcrest area that borders Tulip Avenue, became part of the village in the 1930s. The post–World War II era saw this area rapidly built up with Cape Cod–style houses.

In 1929, an enormous elementary school was constructed in the west end of the village. It was aptly named the Floral–Park Bellerose School and served not only Floral Park, but the Village of Bellerose and Bellerose Terrace. Sewanhaka High School opened in 1930, and Floral Park Memorial High School opened in 1957. The most dramatic change in the post–World War II era came in 1960–1961, when Jericho Turnpike was widened by New York State, causing the demolition of 64 buildings on the north side of the road, plus the elevation of the tracks and railroad station occurred during the same time period. The entire village had to cope with this disruption and modernization of the transportation system.

Due to its location, the efforts of pioneer residents, and sense of community, Floral Park continues into the future as a wonderful place to live and raise a family.

One

HINSDALE BECOMES
FLORAL PARK

Early maps note part of the area where Floral Park is located was known as Plainfield, which in time blended into the area known as East Hinsdale. The Light Horse Road, now known as Tulip Avenue, ran southeast from Jericho Road and was a main path where people could give their steeds a bit of free reign and exercise. The adjoining area to the west was known as Hinsdale. In a survey dated 1849, the land at the center of this area was owned by William Baily, also known as Baylis or Bailiss. On April 30, 1874, the land was conveyed to Egbert Guernsey and George I. Tyson, and the last conveyance of this tract of land was made on July 10, 1889, to John Lewis Childs. The deed at that particular time showed this section was called Plainfield, Town of Hempstead, Queens County, New York. Nassau County was not be created until 1899, when the eastern 70 percent of Queens County would be divided off after Queens became a borough of the City of New York. The Village of Floral Park is in both the Towns of Hempstead and North Hempstead with Jericho Road, later referred to as Jericho Turnpike, State Route 25, dividing the townships. An early train stop was located near the Plainfield Road, which ran north to south at the center of the area. The Long Island Railroad and Central Railroad of New York would be a prominent part of this area that would eventually be named Floral Park, providing both passenger and freight service for the area. Trolley service along Jericho Road would also be a means of transportation in the era predominated by travel by horse and wagon.

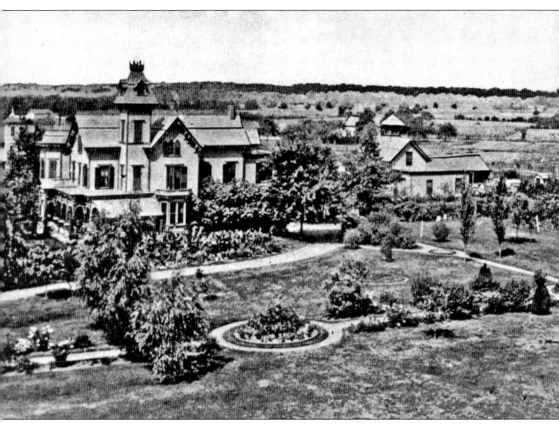

This bird's-eye view of the residence and grounds of John Lewis Childs was published in a booklet he printed in 1893. The vast empty space of the Hempstead plains can be see looking north from the railroad station. Frequent additions were made to Childs's grand home over the decades to house his various collections. He was a great naturalist and collector of bird eggs. He and his wife, Mary Caroline Goldsmith Childs, had four children, Carlton, Vernon, Lionel, and Norma. The mansion survived until 1950, when it was demolished to make way for an apartment complex. By that time, only his daughter Norma Childs Schwieters, her husband, John; and a sister-in-law, Clarice Childs, were living in the 34-room mansion. Upkeep on the wood-frame structure was enormous, and historic preservation of Victorian-era homes would not be prevalent until decades later. (W. Gosden.)

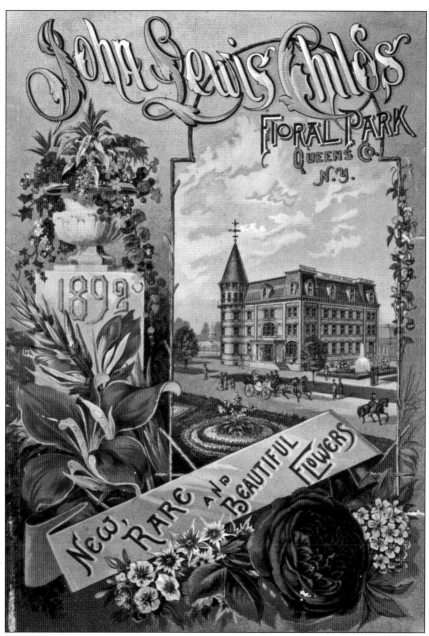

John Lewis Childs issued wonderful illustrated catalogs semiannually offering his immense selection of seeds, bulbs, plants, and vegetables. This image is of the fall catalog for 1892 and shows the fireproof, brick seed house that he had built. The catalogs were printed in Childs's own printing plant, as well as one in Rochester, New York. The color work for the cover and several interior pages was done in Brooklyn by the H. M. Wall Company. In the first run, 400,000 copies of this catalog were printed, and others were printed as needed. To make up the catalogs, 140 tons of paper were required, and a grand total of $84,000 was spent just to produce the entire first print run. The catalog was more than 150 pages, and with postage at 5¢ per copy sent out to customers, the total production cost was $20,000. Childs's operation, just to produce the catalogs, was indeed a huge one. (W. Gosden.)

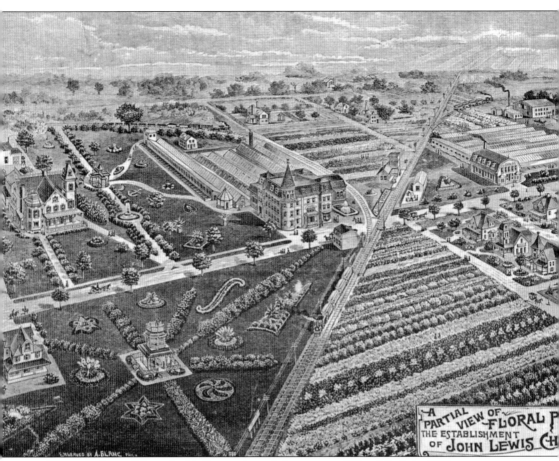

This artist's rendition of a bird's-eye view of the center of Floral Park in 1892 was engraved by A. Blanc of Philadelphia on a special commission by Childs and was featured in his fall seed catalog. It gives a fairly accurate view of the town looking west. At the center is the fireproof seed house with greenhouses behind it; to the left is Childs's mansion. The Long Island Railroad passes to the right of the seed house, and the branch off to the left, just past the seed house, is the Creedmoor spur branch of the New York Central Railroad. At the extreme right edge, at center, is the Methodist Episcopal church with a cross on the lawn (which was actually artistic license, as there never was one). Childs Hall is directly above that, with the greenhouses behind it, and the hall faced Tulip Avenue, which divides the image from left to right. (W. Gosden.)

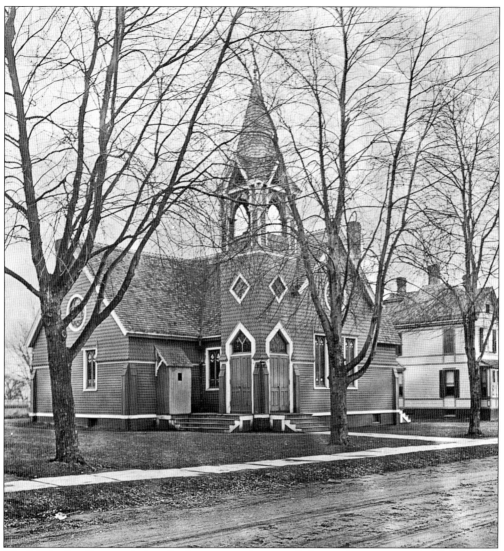

The Methodist Episcopal church, shown in a photograph dating from approximately 1892, was built on land donated by John Lewis Childs. It was the first church in Floral Park and was located on Verbena Avenue. Most of the residents of Floral Park that lived near Tulip Avenue at the center of town were of the Methodist faith. Erection of a masonry building was completed in 1927, and the original wood structure was moved and incorporated into the center of the design of the new church, where it serves as a chapel. It was renamed in 1939 the Floral Park Methodist Church and then, in 1968, the United Methodist Church. The church continues to be a place where many organizations of the village hold their meetings. (FPL.)

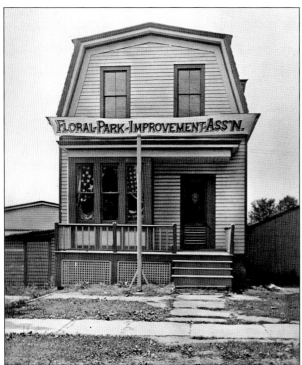

This building was constructed in 1887 and served as the first post office, located on the south side of Tulip Avenue. In about 1890, it was moved to the corner of Tulip and Iris Avenues, where it is pictured here, and it became the office of the Floral Park Improvement Association. It later served as Natillio's Barbershop, the second barber in Floral Park. (FPL.)

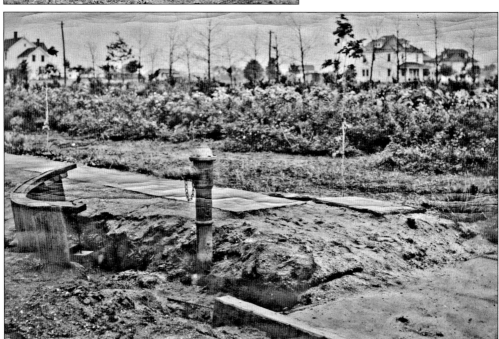

This view shows Violet Avenue looking north toward the center of town in June 1909. The primitive development and installation of paved sidewalks and curbs as the building of new homes proceeded is shown. Small nurseries that were not rivals of John Lewis Childs existed to serve local customers. The nursery stock of Adolpf Jaenicke is thriving on the east side of the road in this photograph. (VFP.)

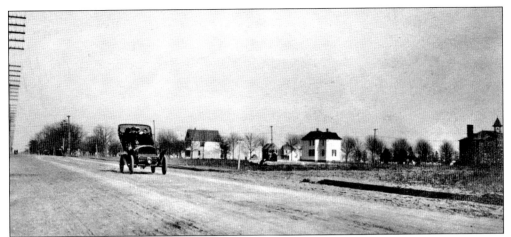

Jericho Turnpike is the major east-west road that runs for miles at the center of Long Island. This photograph was taken around 1905 looking southwest from the location of Belmont Avenue. Floral Park School is on the extreme right, and the trees behind the car note where South Tyson Avenue crosses the turnpike, as well as the location of the old apple orchard. (FPL.)

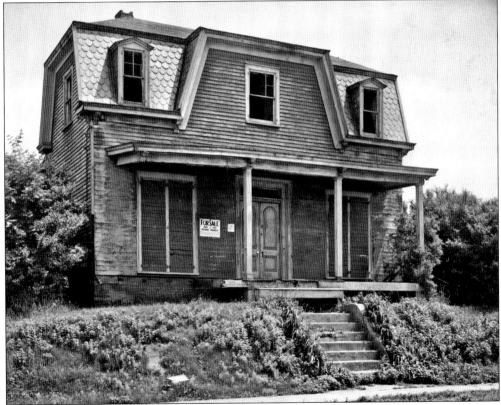

This early residence, at 21 Hemlock Street, was constructed just after the Civil War. By the summer of 1942, when this photograph was taken, it was owned by William Wissback of Poplar Street. The house had not been inhabited for some time and was up for sale. The 100-by-110-foot property would be divided into two building plots, and the house would be demolished soon after. (VFP.)

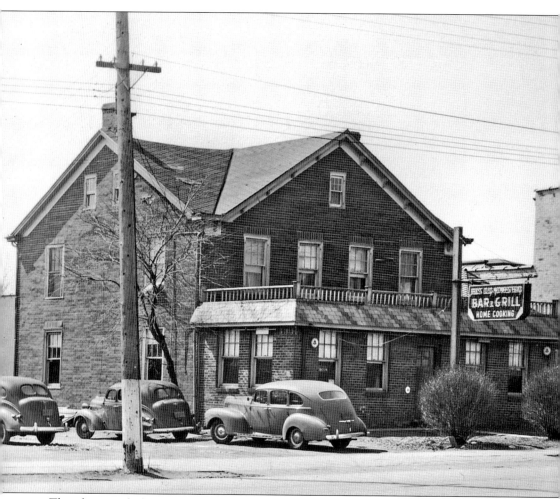

This photograph shows the Homestead Hotel in the late 1930s on Jericho Turnpike. It was owned and operated by one of the earliest families in Floral Park area—the Wicks. They were farmers and owned extensive acreage from Hillside Avenue at the north, continuing out to New Hyde Park on the east and south across Jericho Turnpike and down across the railroad tracks for the branch leading to Mineola. Many members of the Wicks family lived in this building and in the family farmhouse on Little Neck Road. This hotel served many weary travelers in the area before motorized transportation. The Wicks also owned a similar establishment in New Hyde Park 1 mile farther east. The property the Wicks owned between the Mineola and Hempstead branch railroad tracks at the Floral Park–New Hyde Park border was sold to the village for a playground area and ball fields in the 1920s. (VFP.)

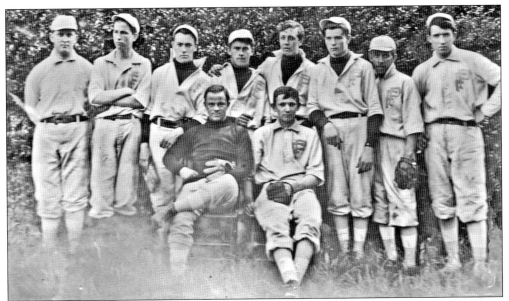

Baseball has always been a favorite sport in Floral Park, as this c. 1904 photograph shows. The fields used to play ball were located just southeast of the train station and Tulip Avenue. In this image are, from left to right, (seated) Sylvester Tuthill and ? Mulcahey; (standing) Linn Allen, Harry Allen, Vernon Childs, Neil Pike, Royden Klein, William Umstadt, Abbot the Rabbit, and ? Flynn. (FPL.)

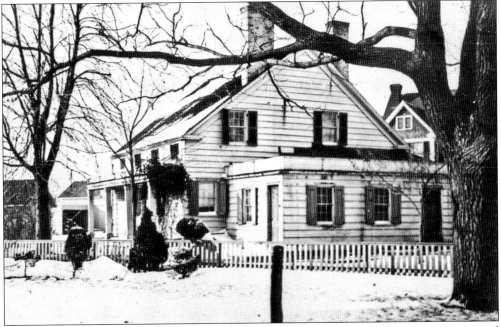

The oldest house in Floral Park was home to the Baylis family for many decades. It is pictured here on Carnation Avenue. The Baylis family owned a large area of land starting at Carnation Avenue and proceeding west, following the Long Island Railroad tracks. Additions have expanded the dwelling, and builder and former mayor John McNeil reworked the interior to a great extent in the 1920s. (VFP.)

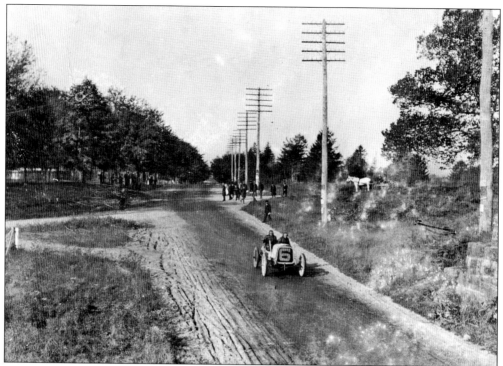

The first international road race for the William K. Vanderbilt Jr. Cup took place in 1904. This photograph shows the race in progress as a car speeds through Floral Park. The car is a Pope-Toledo driven by Herbert Lyte. This race is the most famous road race on Long Island and in New York. (VFP.)

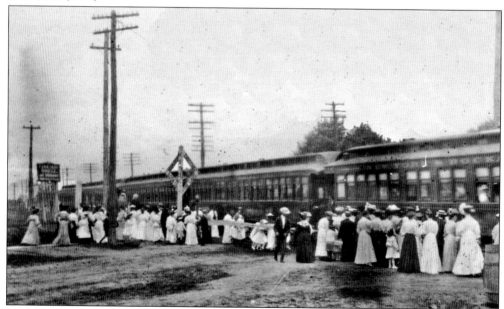

It is likely the crowd waiting to board the train is headed east to the Mineola Fair. The fair started at the end of the Civil War and was an annual showcase for farmers' produce and livestock. It was so important that schools were closed so all could attend. (VFP.)

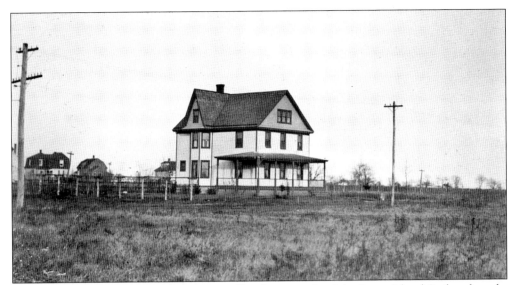

The Meagher property was a large tract of land just south of the Long Island Railroad tracks and east of Plainfield Avenue. This photograph shows the home of Wallace Thurston, who was postmaster of Floral Park from 1924 to 1932. The Thurston family had four sons: the youngest, Bryan, was killed in World War I, and another son, Bruce, was a charter member of the local Republican Committee, started in 1933. (VFP.)

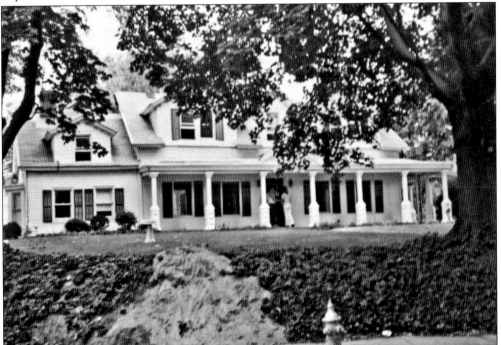

The L. K. Suydam family had a large farmhouse and plot of land on the west side of Plainfield Avenue. Three large barns were at the back of the property, and it was an active farm into the 20th century. This photograph was taken around 1955. The land was eventually sold for development, and after a devastating fire destroyed half of the home, it was demolished around 1971. (VFP.)

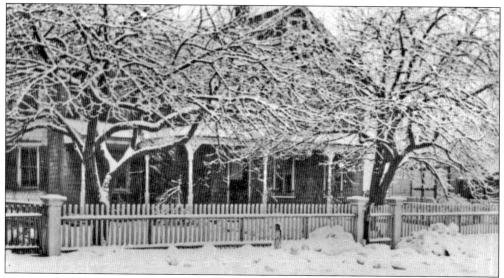

Shown in the above photograph is the home of "Aunt Hanna" Chisholm, an African American woman who owned a large piece of property on the corner of Carnation and Atlantic Avenues. She purchased the property, which had a house and several barns on it, about 1903. Aunt Hanna was held in high regard by the people who lived and worked in Floral Park. She also was a foster parent to numerous African American children. In the photograph below are, from left to right, Albert Thurston, Ed Hicks, and Harry Allen. Ed Hicks and his younger sister, Bertha, were part of Aunt Hanna's family and attended the Floral Park School, where they were well known to everyone. (Both, VFP.)

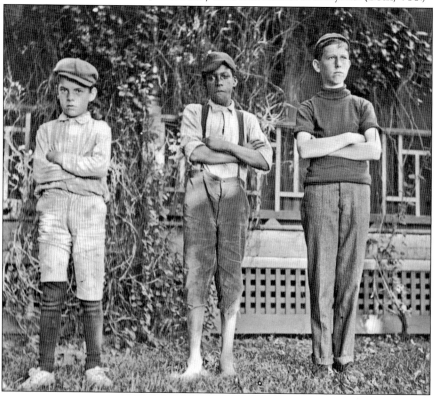

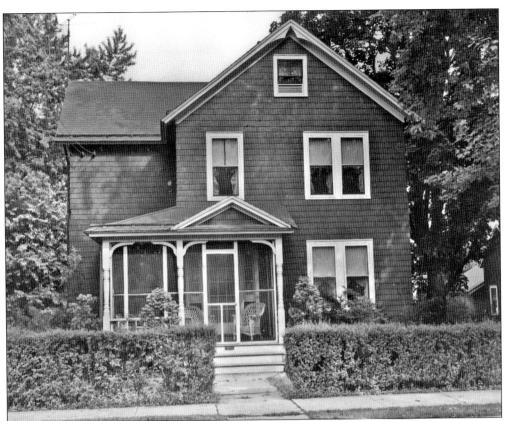

The Downing family home (pictured above) was on Verbena Avenue, a few houses south of the Methodist church. George H. Downing was active in the village as a trustee, president (1919–1921) and member of the school board (1922–1930). He worked for the post office until 1910, when he became president of the Titus Brown Lumber Company in the city of Glen Cove. His mother, Sara Hurd, came to this area in 1861 from Oxford, Massachusetts, to teach school at Public School No. 8, on Jericho Turnpike, as its first teacher. Downing remained active in village affairs until his demise in October 1957, when he was a member of the Historical Committee for the 50th anniversary of Floral Park. The photograph at right shows George Downing in later life. (Both, VFP.)

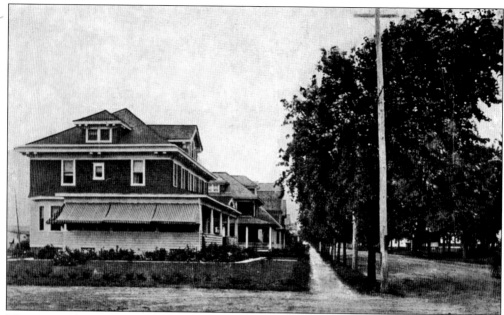

This postcard of the Stattle residence most likely spelled the family name wrong when it was printed. Telephone books later spelled the name as Stattel, and by 1939, George Stattel, who owned the Long Island Steel Company, lived at the address 39 Emerson Avenue. The Stattel family owned a large farm on the Little Neck Road from 1892 to 1926. (FPL.)

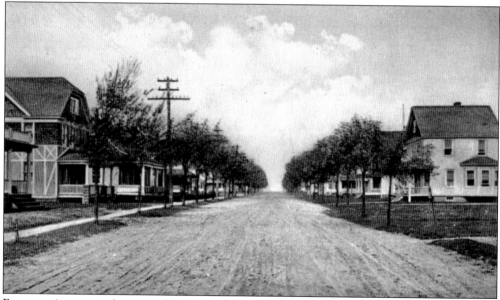

Emerson Avenue is shown in this postcard view looking north at a point just beyond Lowell Avenue. This area of the village is in the Town of North Hempstead. Note the dirt road and that sidewalks are only on the west side of the road. Most of the houses in this image were newly constructed, as all lack significant plants and shrubbery. (FPL.)

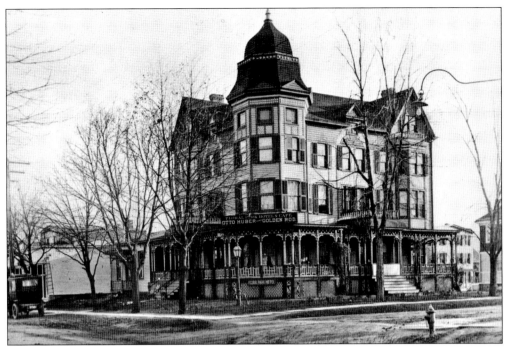

The Park House was built in 1890 by John Lewis Childs as a residence for his employees. It became the Floral Park Hotel and Café by 1918 and, by 1906, was sold to Fred Schmensing, who also owned all the property on the south side of Tulip Avenue between Violet and Iris Avenues. The hotel lasted until 1928–1929. (FPL.)

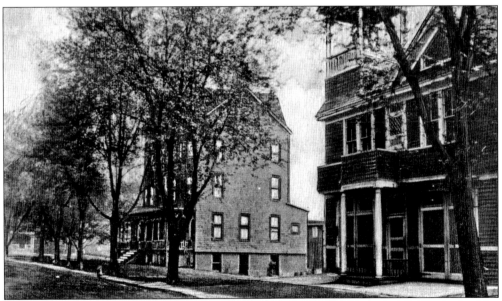

The northeast side of Violet Avenue is shown in this postcard, from around 1912. The back of the Floral Park Hotel, built as the Park House by John Lewis Childs in 1890, is shown next to the Fireman's Hall, which was built in 1901. Seen in the distance at the far left is the Woodbine Apartment House that was created by converting the former Childs gladiolus bulb house. (FPL.)

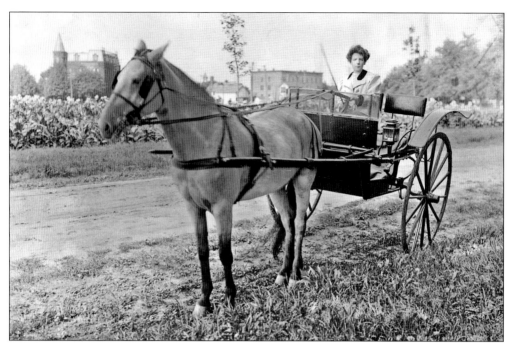

With a field of flowers in bloom behind her, Aline Shute is in charge of the latest in stylish transportation for 1895. This photograph is from the north end of Floral Boulevard. In the background is one of the largest brick structures of the time, the Childs seed warehouse. At the center of the photograph are the Tyson apartments and office building, which still exist. (VFP.)

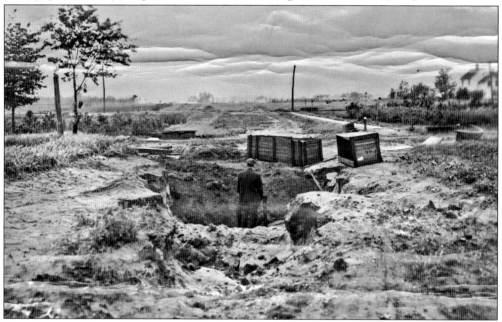

This photograph shows the corner of Clarence and Violet Avenues looking southeast. The western edge of the Hempstead Plains is still evident, with empty fields and faint images of houses in the distance, half a mile or more away. Vast areas of land were still undeveloped, and street patterns were just starting to take place within a five-minute walk from the center of town. (FPHS.)

Two

FLORISTS AND SEEDSMEN

Acres of flowers lined the south side of the Long Island Railroad tracks for more than 1 mile, from the extreme western border of Floral Park to the center of town 1 mile away. The passenger trains would slow down when the flowers were in full bloom so their passengers could take in the amazing view. The Central Railroad of New York was owned by Alexander T. Stewart, who built the planned community of Garden City 3 miles east of Floral Park. It merged into the Long Island Railroad at the center of Floral Park, and upon Stewart's demise, the Central Railroad was purchased by the rival Long Island Railroad. The Hinsdale train station was on Stewart's line, just north of Jericho Road in an area before Creed's farm, which would eventually lend its name to that line of track referred to as the Creedmoor spur. John Lewis Childs realized that rail service would be the way he would transport essential material to his business, from the paper for his printing plant to the mail sent to and from the post office he established near his business to serve his ever-growing customer list, which extended well beyond the shores of the United States. Most of the other florists and seedsmen in Floral Park were suppliers to local customers. The annual or semiannual seed catalogs were issued on a regular basis by Childs, John Roscoe Fuller, and Mary E. Martin. Fuller was the brother-in-law of John Childs and lived right next to him, and he also had his greenhouses at the back of his property. Mary Martin had her business on Jericho Road about 1 mile away. She was one of the few single women with her own business of any kind in that era with customers beyond the immediate area.

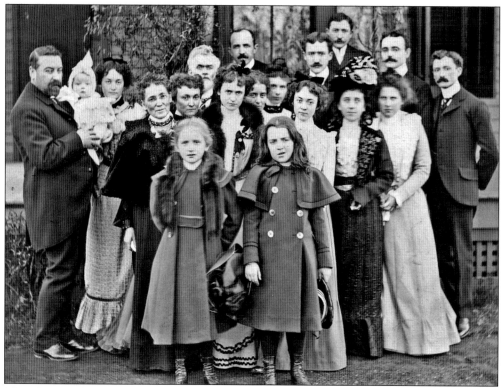

This photograph, dating from approximately 1900, shows the Childs and Goldsmith families. John Lewis Childs is on the far left, and Arthur Goldsmith, his brother-in-law, is on the far right. Mary Caroline Goldsmith Childs is standing directly behind the young blond girl with the fur collar, and it is believed that Julia Norris Goldsmith, Mary Caroline's mother, is to the left. (VFP.)

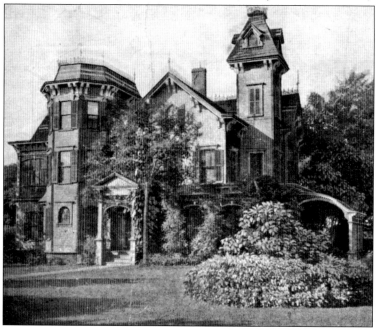

The residence of John Lewis Childs was by far one of the finest and, indeed, the largest house for miles around. It was built in approximately 1882, and Childs was living there when he married in 1886 at age 30. It accommodated Childs and his family, as well as his enormous collection and library of birds of North America. (FPL.)

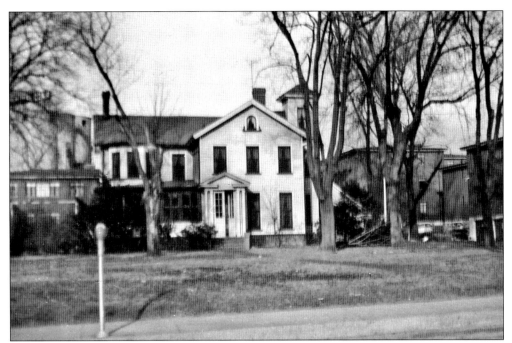

John Roscoe Fuller's home was built before 1900 and was located on Tulip Avenue next to his brother-in-law, John Lewis Childs. Fuller was married to Childs's sister and was also in the seed, bulb, and plant business. He issued his own catalogs and sold locally or by mail order. (VFP.)

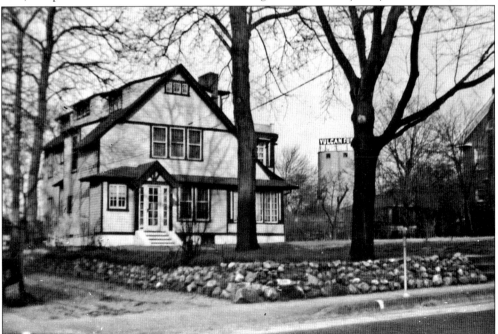

This home was built prior to World War I on the northwest end of Tulip Avenue. It was owned by a Mr. Herbert, who was a plumbing contractor. It was one of three homes that were built on the north side of Tulip Avenue between Jericho Turnpike and the train station. The house was demolished in 1964 to make way for the new post office. (VFP.)

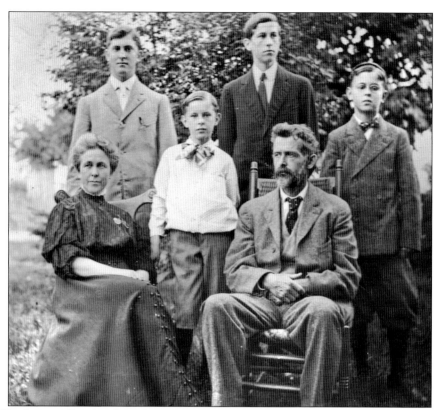

The Charles H. Allen family is shown in this 1905 photograph. Pictured from left to right are (seated) Mrs. Allen and Charles H. Allen, who was the son of Charles Linnaeus Allen; (standing) Linn, Philip, Harry, and Irving. Following in his father's footsteps, Charles H. Allen had a nursery and seed business, located on the north side of Jericho Turnpike, just east of Tyson Avenue, about where Whitney Avenue is today. Around 1900, the Allen family moved to a house on the southwest corner of Carnation and Crocus Avenues. He sold the Jericho Turnpike establishment to Joel and Rena Hayden. Charles Allen had a processing plant and greenhouses for a nursery business on the north side of Verbena Avenue between Floral Boulevard and Carnation Avenue, as shown in the photograph below, dating from 1909. (Both, FPL.)

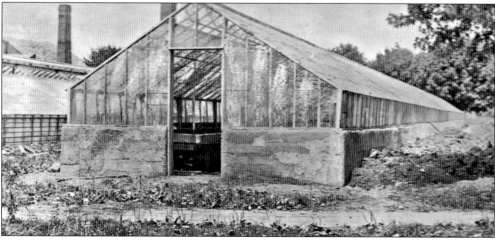

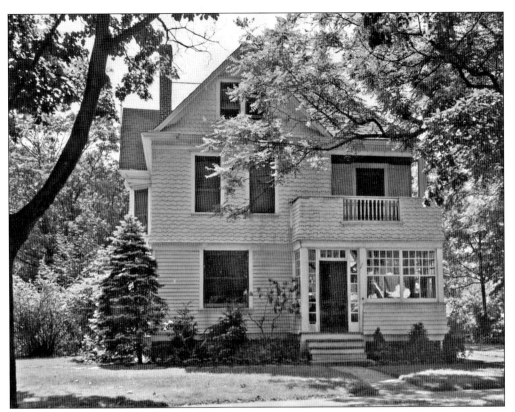

This photograph shows the Charles H. Allen home. Charles Allen's father was the florist and seedsman that John Lewis Childs wrote to seeking work. The Allen home was built prior to 1900 and stood opposite his nursery and greenhouses, which were built on a triangular-shaped piece of property bordered by Carnation and Verbena Avenues and Floral Boulevard. The house, although modified, still exists to this day. (FPL.)

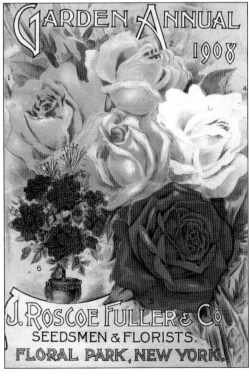

The cover shown for this *Garden Annual* from 1908 was from J. Roscoe Fuller's Company. Fuller had his seed and florist business in Floral Park during the 1880–1910 era on Tulip Avenue behind his house. He had no other property or buildings for his business or investments in real estate like other merchants in the area, yet he was quite prosperous. (W. Gosden.)

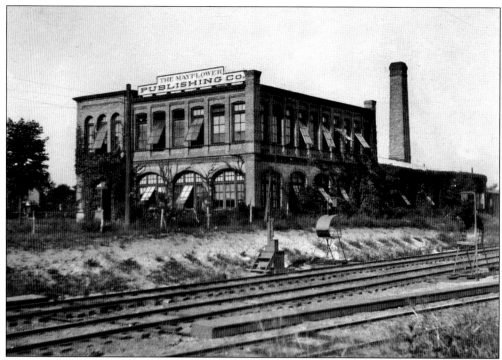

The Mayflower Publishing Company building, shown in the photograph above, was built by John Lewis Childs around 1886 on South Tyson Avenue next to the railroad tracks. Its location allowed for large quantities of paper to be unloaded when it arrived by rail in freight cars. Childs printed his seed catalogs; newspapers, the *Island* and the *Nassau Event*; a monthly magazine, the *Mayflower*; and other publications here. At the height of his business, he was printing nearly half a million catalogs twice a year, which were mailed worldwide. Decades later, the local paper, the *Gateway*, was printed here as well. When it ceased being used as a print shop, the building was converted into the home of the Ajax Building and Roofing Supply Company. The building was demolished in 1960 when the railroad tracks and train station were elevated. (Both, FPL.)

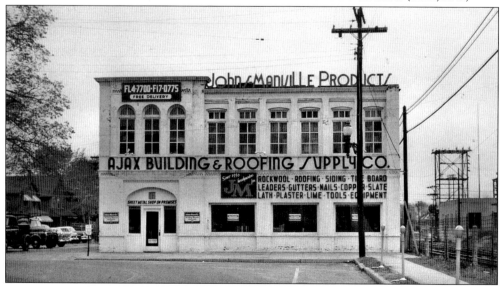

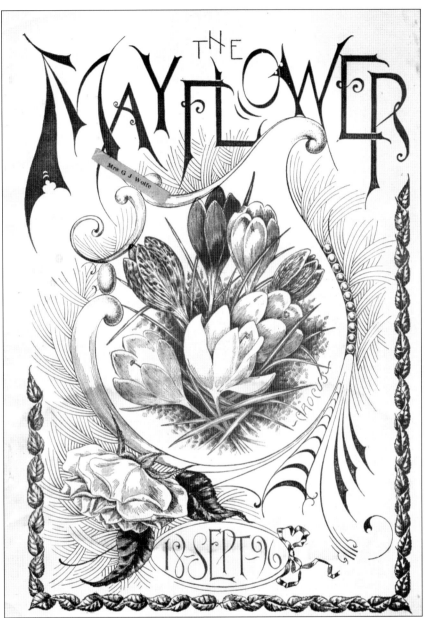

This cover is from John Lewis Childs's *Mayflower* magazine for September 1896. He had been printing and publishing his own monthly magazine since 1884. The subscription price was 50¢ a year, and the magazine was devoted to the cultivation of flowers, plants, fruits, and vegetables, and to gardening and home adornment in general. This particular issue saw 275,000 copies sent worldwide to subscribers. Childs, always the great promoter, would send 20 bulbs to all who subscribed or renewed each year. At least one full-color plate was in each issue, and occasionally, color covers were used as well. A series of articles with the title "Nature's Series" were authored by Charles L. Allen, who was the man that Childs first worked for when he arrived in the area in 1874. Subscribers' articles and comments were printed in each issue. The issues carried some small advertisements in the back pages for everything from hairpins, to "true blood purifiers," boot polish, and secondhand bicycles. (W. Gosden.)

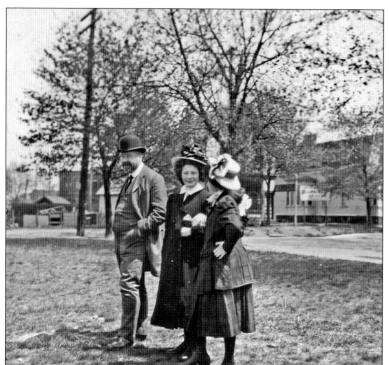

With Tulip Avenue and Verbena Avenue in the back, John Lewis Childs is seen standing at the edge of his property awaiting the start of a baseball game with two unidentified ladies. The games took place on Sunday afternoons, and Childs donated funds for the teams to have uniforms with Floral Park lettered on them when they began to compete against other teams. (VFP.)

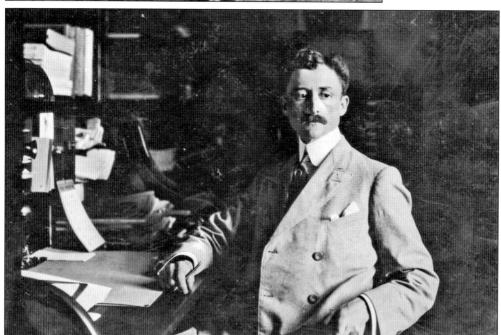

The Goldsmith family was from Washingtonville in Orange County. Mary Caroline Goldsmith, daughter of Rienzi and Julia Goldsmith, married John Lewis Childs on April 15, 1886, and moved to Floral Park. Arthur Goldsmith, shown here, was the brother of Mary Caroline Childs. Goldsmith became the manager at the Childs's seed and bulb business, and bought property in Floral Park. (FPL.)

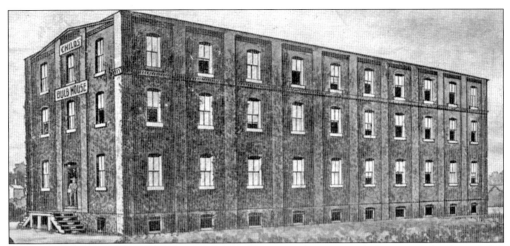

The bulb warehouse of John Lewis Childs, shown in the postcard above, was built in 1885. Childs's business was growing rapidly, and separate buildings to house bulbs and seeds were required. The warehouses were used to store what was grown in the fields and cultivated in the greenhouses. (FPL.)

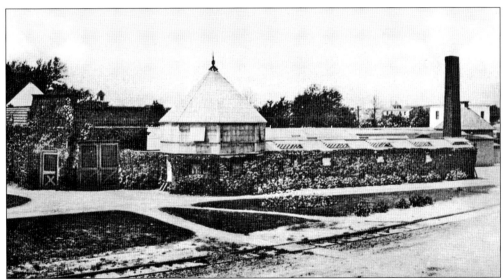

The greenhouses of Childs's business were extensive, covering many acres. Section I, pictured above in a postcard from the mid-1890s, also shows the single track of the Central Railroad of New York in the foreground. This line cut through the center of Childs's operations and existed before he arrived on Long Island. By the time this card was issued, the Long Island Railroad had leased the track. (FPL.)

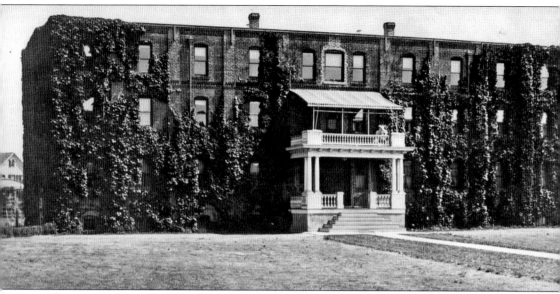

This image shows the Woodbine Court Apartment House around 1912. By the time of the incorporation of the village in 1908, John Lewis Childs had been dividing and selling the fields where he raised flowers into building lots. The bulb house built in 1885 was remodeled into this apartment house, with the division of the floor space into apartments and the addition of an entrance at the center of the south side of the building. The basic shape and structure of the building remained the same, but as the decades passed, it saw several transformations. The vast lawn seen in this photograph and the garden to the left would be eliminated when a crescent-shaped road would be cut through from Plainfield Avenue to connect to Violet Avenue. At the front, metal fire escapes would be added to flank the entrance, which would also be remodeled to have an open porch on all three stories. The building was demolished in 1960 when the train tracks were elevated. (FPL.)

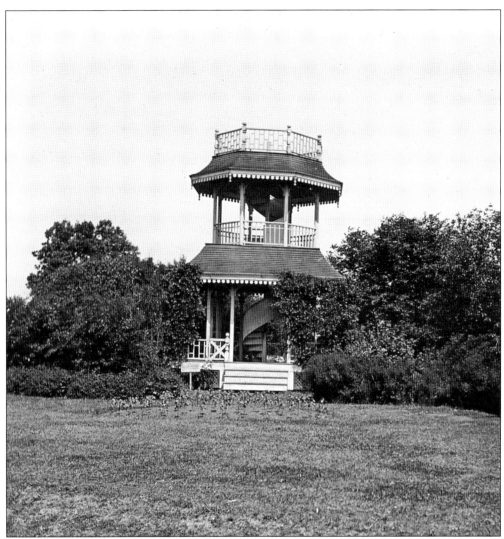

John Lewis Childs had a huge park and garden area planted directly across from his mansion on the south side of Tulip Avenue. Among its features was a huge two-story, Japanese-styled pagoda, as shown in this image from around 1890. It was nearly new when this photograph was taken, and the spiral staircase at the center can be clearly seen. It was located just north of the train station. The pagoda, along with the castle-like seed house opposite it, would become landmarks for the train passengers as they arrived and traveled through Floral Park. Childs had the pagoda built across from his house so that it would be the first thing seen when stepping out. It was a wonderful setting but, like all wood structures, required a large amount of maintenance to keep it looking fresh. It was torn down in 1915 after deteriorating structurally. (FPL.)

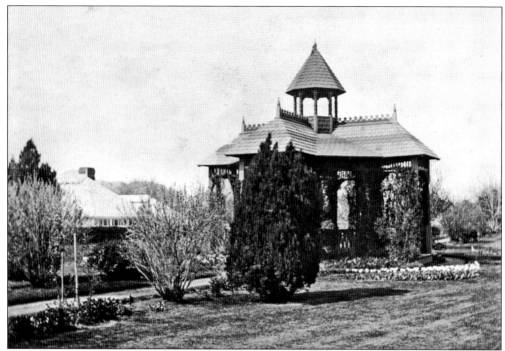

The property surrounding the Childs mansion had many buildings on it. The summerhouse was built in the shape of a cross with a small tower at the center. It was located in the extensive lawn area, with the main greenhouse building to its south. The four Childs children used it as a playhouse, especially daughter Norma. (FPL.)

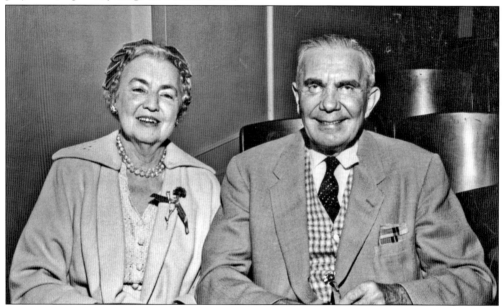

This photograph, taken in 1958, shows Norma and John Schweiters. Norma Dee Childs was the only daughter of John Lewis and Mary Caroline Childs. Norma outlived her three brothers and would move into one wing of the Childs mansion in an apartment with her husband, John Schwieters. (VFP.)

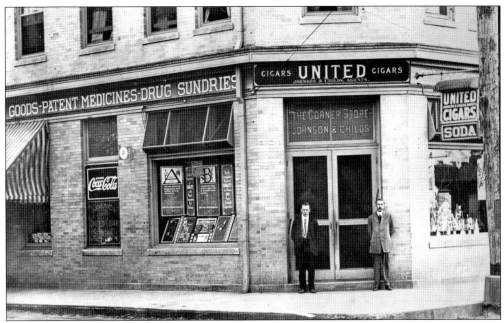

The photograph above shows Vernon Childs (left) and Edgar Johnson in front of their store, next to the Tulip Avenue railroad crossing. Vernon Childs was the son of John Lewis Childs, on whose property the building was constructed in 1909. They sold cigars, soda, patent medicines, and drug sundries. The photograph below shows Edward A. Ullman and his family, who rented the southwest corner for a confectionery store. The Ullmans purchased a building plot for a home on Elizabeth Street, near the Floral Park School, in 1906 from the House and Home Company. By 1908, they were in their home and, by 1910, had established their business. Ullman eventually took over the Corner Store from Johnson and Childs. (Above, FPL; below, VFP.)

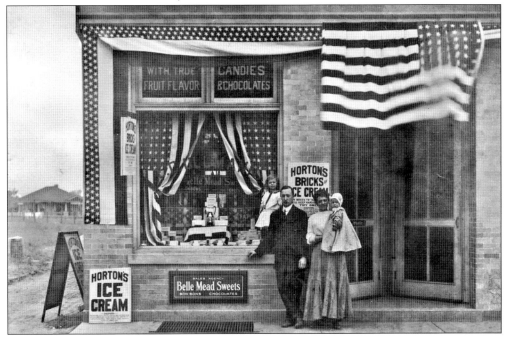

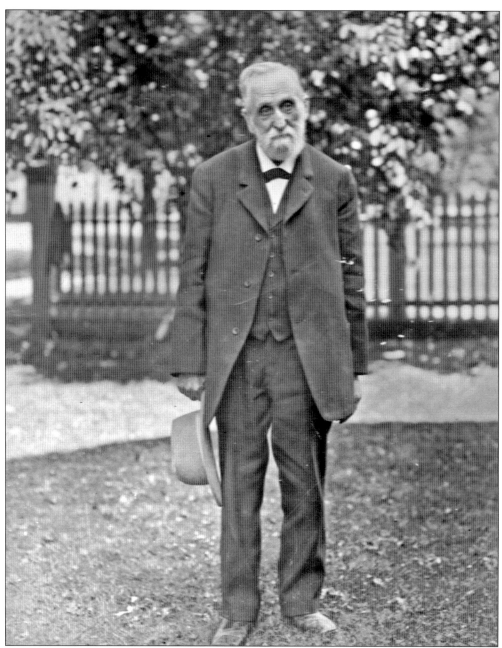

Charles Linnaeus Allen was a florist in Hinsdale with a business and property on the northwest corner of Jericho Turnpike and Little Neck Road. John Lewis Childs of Maine wrote to him in 1874 to request employment and was told to come down, at which point he was hired. After a year, Childs went out on his own and prospered. Allen, at least as early as 1868–1869, had a business in Brooklyn at the corner of Columbia and Doughty Streets, noting he was an importer and dealer in all kinds of flowering bulbs and seeds. He was using Brooklyn as a base of operation when he moved to what would be eventually referred to as Floral Park. His home was on the northeast corner of South Tyson Avenue and Mayflower Place, and in his later years, he would walk the short distance to the Floral Park School to talk to the children about horticulture. (FPL.)

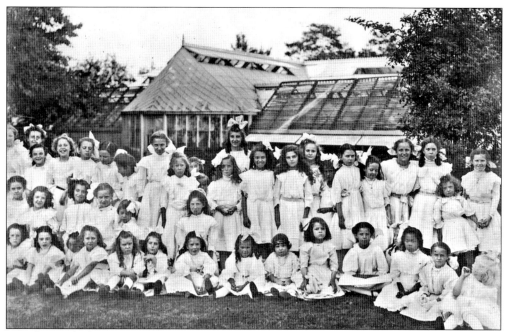

A tradition of John Lewis Childs was to host a garden party for all of the children in the community on the lawn of his home. One hundred invitations were sent out, and refreshments, games, and entertainment were provided. Shown in the photograph above from around 1905 is one of the parties, and Bertha Hicks is in the first row, third from the right. (FPL.)

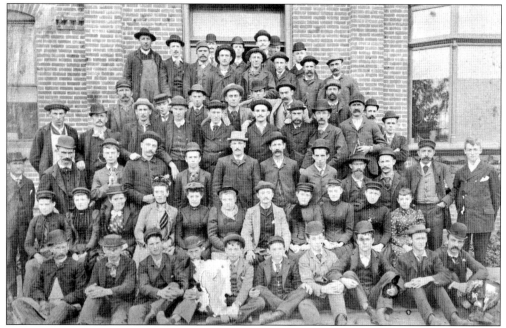

Dating from 1895, this photograph shows some of the employees of John Lewis Childs when his business was at its peak. They are gathered on the front steps of the fireproof seed house, which was built in 1890. Many of the workers resided in attached houses, an apartment house, or at the hotel built and owned by Childs. Other employees lived in the surrounding communities. (FPL.)

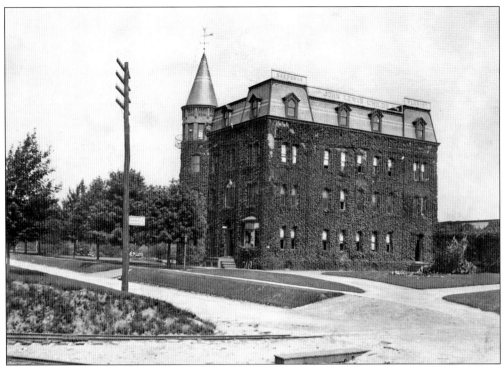

The four-story, fireproof seed warehouse was an immense, fortress-like, brick building located just south of the Childs mansion. It was erected in 1890 and could be seen from great distances. At the top of the tower was a studio space, where Childs employed an artist full time to illustrate his catalogs, seed packets, and magazine. This photograph shows the structure when it was approximately five years old. (FPL.)

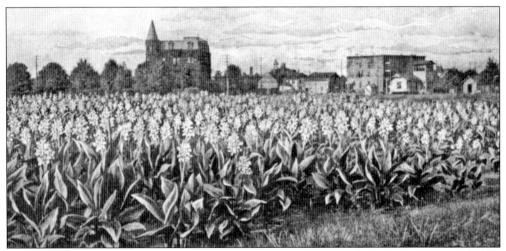

This postcard view shows a small part of the vast acres of flowers that were grown on Childs's property. The acres of flowers extended west for 1 mile and were considered a great attraction to see when riding on the train. The seeds from these flowers were harvested and processed, packaged, and stored for shipment in the brick seed house. (FPL.)

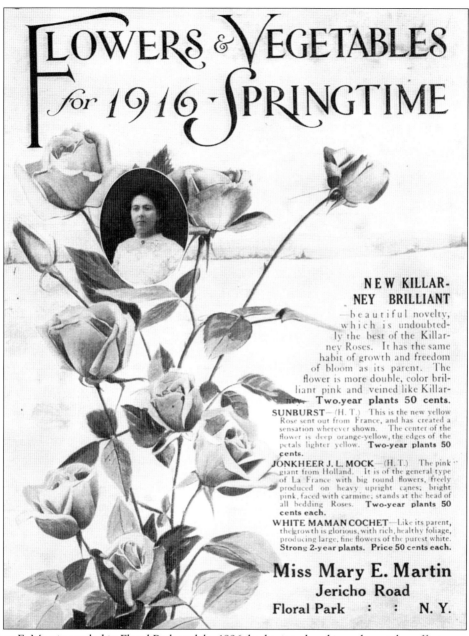

FLOWERS & VEGETABLES for 1916 · SPRINGTIME

NEW KILLAR-NEY BRILLIANT—beautiful novelty, which is undoubtedly the best of the Killarney Roses. It has the same habit of growth and freedom of bloom as its parent. The flower is more double, color brilliant pink and veined like Killarney. **Two-year plants 50 cents.**

SUNBURST—(H. T.) This is the new yellow Rose sent out from France, and has created a sensation wherever shown. The center of the flower is deep orange-yellow, the edges of the petals lighter yellow. **Two-year plants 50 cents.**

JONKHEER J. L. MOCK—(H. T.) The pink giant from Holland. It is of the general type of La France with big round flowers, freely produced on heavy upright canes; bright pink, faced with carmine; stands at the head of all bedding Roses. **Two-year plants 50 cents each.**

WHITE MAMAN COCHET—Like its parent, the growth is glorious, with rich, healthy foliage, producing large, fine flowers of the purest white. **Strong 2-year plants. Price 50 cents each.**

Miss Mary E. Martin
Jericho Road
Floral Park : : N. Y.

Mary E. Martin settled in Floral Park and, by 1896, had printed and issued a catalog offering seeds for flowers and vegetables for sale by mail order. Her property was located on Jericho Road, where Hawthorne Avenue is now located. She was an early advocate of healthful foods and noted in her 1913 catalog, "Food and proper environment shape the human race more then anything else. Meat eating alone tends strongly to savagery." She was more than ahead of her time as a female, as there were few single independent businesswomen in that era. She stated that, in order to be happy, people had to be willing to "heed the cry, Back to Nature." Mary Martin also reminded her customers in every catalog she issued that she was in no way connected with any other seed or floral establishment doing business at Floral Park. She stayed in business until approximately World War I and died in 1932 in Floral Park. (W. Gosden.)

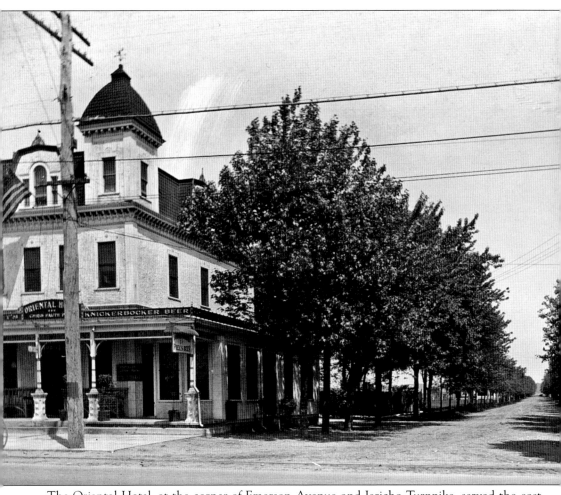

The Oriental Hotel, at the corner of Emerson Avenue and Jericho Turnpike, served the east border of Floral Park and was in the town of North Hempstead. The hotel, restaurant, bar, and café served as a place for travelers to stay on their journey along the Jericho Turnpike. In 1910, when this photograph was taken, the proprietor was Chris Fauth, who offered beer by Piels, Knickerbocker, and Rupert. In later years, it was known as Rudolph's Tavern, after proprietor Fritz Rudolph. When Prohibition was enacted, it was hard for the tavern owner, Rudolph, to comply with the law and still stay in business. He started to make bootleg beer in a hidden room within the hotel, and local patrons would bring an empty pail in to have it filled, pay for it, and take it home. William Dickson recalled Rudolph was warned to stop two or three times by the police and was finally arrested and went to jail for a year. The building was torn down when the road was widened in 1960. (VFP.)

Three

PROSPEROUS TIMES

There is no denying that John Lewis Childs's arrival from Jay, Maine, in 1874 would be the turning point in the development of this area from a small rural area to a thriving community that would be the foundation for a village 34 years later. In a short period of time, Childs established a major post office, built numerous buildings and dwellings, employed hundreds of people, and helped the local school, fire department, and the first church in the area. Due credit must also be given to early property owners and families such as the Wright, Covert, Wicks, Baylis, Heidtmann, Rose, and Krug families, who all played an important part in the development of the area John Lewis Childs named Floral Park.

Houses of worship have always been the center of the community and village. The Methodist church was the first to be established in 1891 at the center of the village on Verbena Avenue. In 1902, St. Hedwigs Roman Catholic Church was built at the east end of the village to serve the largely Polish-speaking residents of that area, many of whom were employed by John Lewis Childs.

The fire department, established in 1893 as Hook and Ladder Company No. 1, was a fire district that built its own building, which would serve the department's needs as well as providing a meeting place for numerous local organizations. The Floral Park Women's Club was founded in 1898 by a group of prominent ladies, including Mary Caroline Childs. Social activities took place in Childs Hall, which had formerly been an early seed warehouse.

Floral Park became known by word of mouth as passengers on the railroad spread tales of a beautiful place they saw so close to Manhattan. Childs's vast mailings of catalogs also touted the area, and the name of Floral Park became known worldwide to those interested in horticulture.

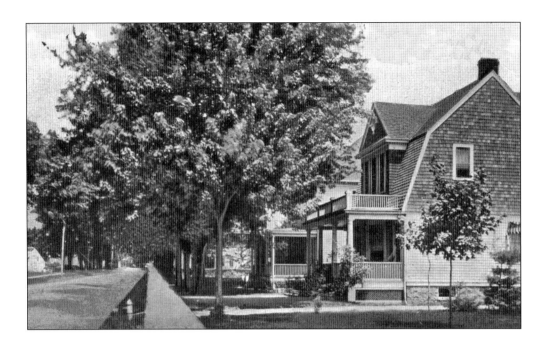

One of the earliest areas to see houses built in Floral Park was where Carnation and Verbena Avenues intersect. The postcard above shows Verbena Avenue looking north from Carnation Avenue. The first house was owned by George Hurrell, who was an active real estate agent that promoted the sale of building lots in the immediate area. The postcard below is Carnation Avenue looking north from the intersection of Verbena and Crocus Avenues. The house at the curve next to the sidewalk is the oldest house in Floral Park, owned for years by the Baylis family. The large house to the right was the residence of Arthur W. Goldsmith, who was Childs brother-in-law and an important part of the Childs seed business. The Goldsmith home was demolished in 1969. (Both, FPL.)

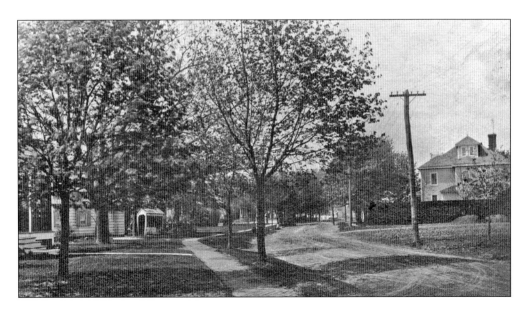

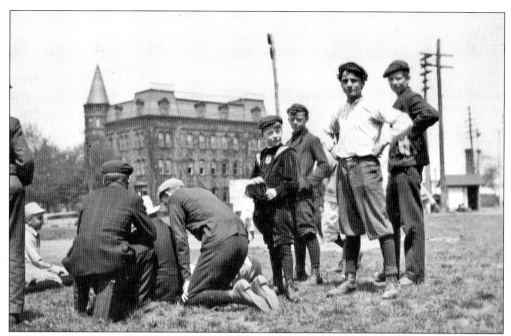

This *c.* 1900 photograph shows the baseball field near the train station. This was the first of several baseball diamonds located on property owned by Childs. As the land that was closest to the main roads was built upon, the ball fields were relocated to other vacant property, and most were near Tulip Avenue. The boy in the center of the photograph is Vernon Childs. (VFP.)

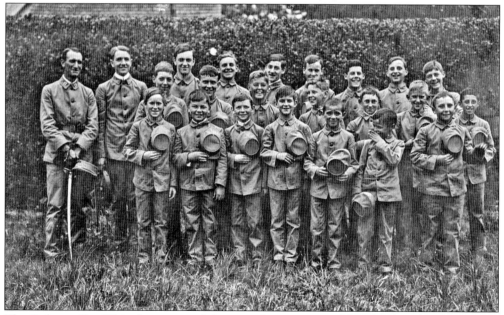

The Cadets or Boys' Brigade was an early boys youth organization. This photograph, taken around 1910, shows Capt. Harry J. Parry at far left, with Lt. Harold Thurston next to him. The group's uniforms resembled those worn by Civil War troops. The Boys' Brigade met in the Methodist church, where Parry was active. By 1914, Floral Park had a Boy Scout troop, and the Boys' Brigade was disbanded. (FPL.)

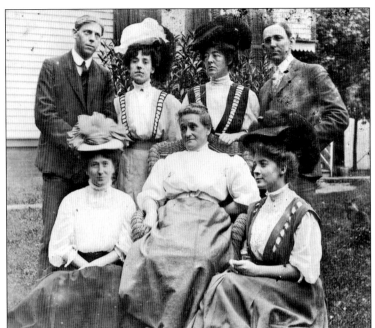

This c. 1907 photograph is of several of the early teachers at Floral Park School No. 22. From left to right are (sitting) C. Evelyn Crooker, Elma Tuthill, and Augusta King (later Mrs. Hugh Davis); (second row) George and Ella Downing (not teachers but Mr. Downing would become a member of the school board in 1922), Ava Hawley, and Henry Davies. (FPL.)

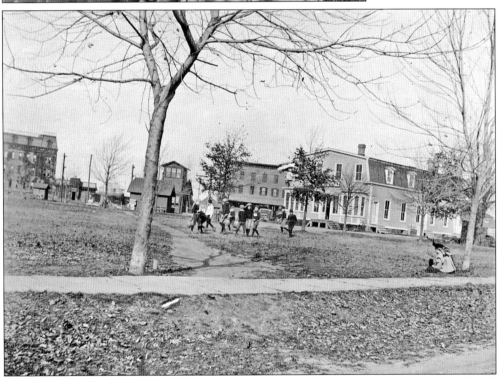

Boys play a game of kickball on the Childs property south of Tulip Avenue between the railroad tracks and Verbena Avenue, which is shown in the foreground. The buildings in the background are, from left to right, the fireproof seed house, built in 1890; the train station (behind the tree); the Tyson Building on the Tyson Block, built in 1894; and Childs Hall, which faces south on Tulip Avenue. (FPL.)

The Wright family is a longtime Floral Park family. This c. 1956 photograph is of Henry Wright Jr., who, with his father, operated a general store in the Tyson Building. They also occupied the large barn at the back of the property for a feed and hay business. Wright operated the first telephone switchboard in the back of the store. (FPL.)

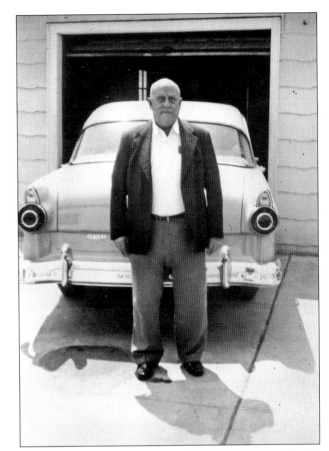

The small building at the corner of Verbena Avenue existed for a brief time and was the real estate office of George Hurrell. By 1906, Childs had started to divide his property closest to the center of town into building lots, and George Hurrell was his agent. (VFP.)

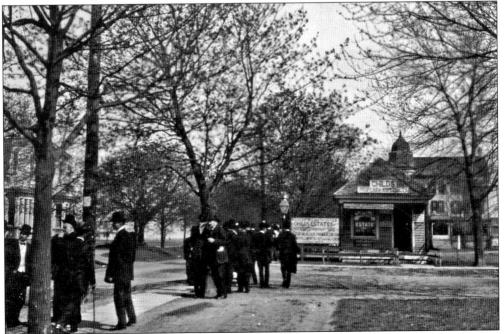

49

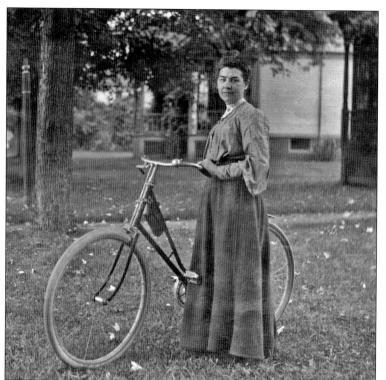

This photograph shows Mrs. William Newton Bird with her bicycle in front of her home on Verbena Avenue. William Bird took the photograph of his wife, as well as many images of the early days of Floral Park, which are now part of the village collection. He was one of Childs's executive employees and, prior to 1910, was active in the fire department, school, and Methodist church. (VFP.)

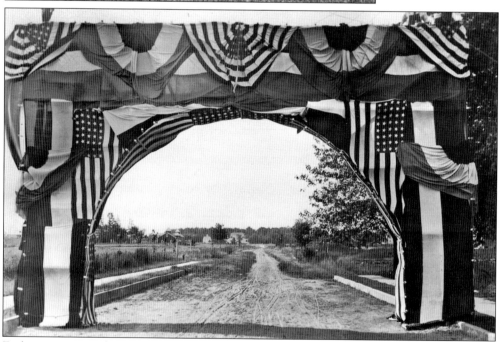

Each year an annual Fireman's Day celebration took place and was a cause of great celebration for the entire community. This c. 1909 image shows the elaborate arch constructed over Violet Avenue between Carnation and Rose Avenues. It was built by Wesley B. Simpson just beyond his own house. (VFP.)

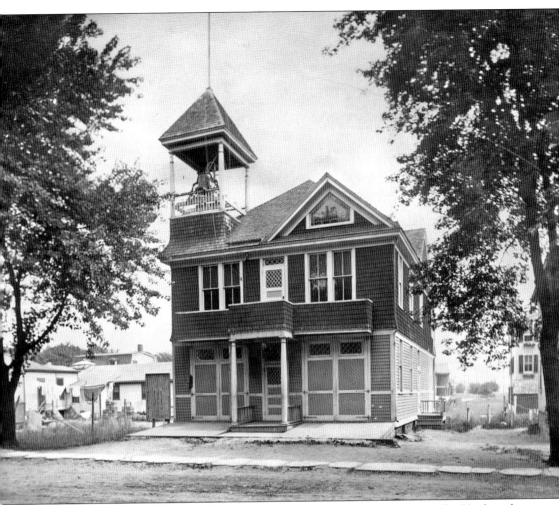

The Floral Park Fire Department was the first organization in the community. The Hook and Ladder Company No. 1 was incorporated in May 1893. At that time, there were fire districts, and funds to sustain the company were obtained by contributions and dues. In 1901, New York State contributed $1,000, and that was the same year the building in the photograph shown here was constructed. On the second floor was a large, furnished meeting room, which not only served the firefighters, but also was used by many other organizations and groups that had formed by that time. The structure was located on Violet Avenue, just south of Tulip Avenue behind the Park House Hotel. The building was sold in 1907, and a little over a year later it was purchased by the newly formed Village of Floral Park. The top floor housed the village offices until 1936, when the new village hall was completed one block away. This property is now the municipal parking lot for the stores along Tulip Avenue. (FPV.)

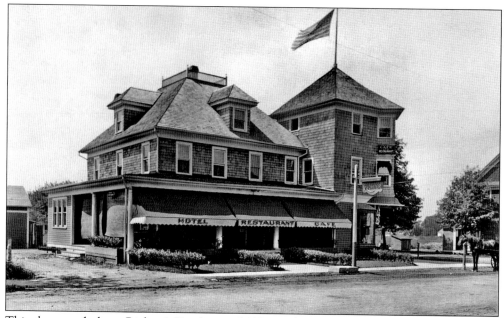

This photograph shows Richter's Hotel around 1900 on the southwest corner of Jericho Turnpike and Tyson Avenue. This hotel featured a café and restaurant, as well as overnight accommodations. It was a popular stop on the trolley line that ran from Jamaica, Queens, to Mineola in Nassau County. Establishments similar to this one were in every town along the dirt-paved Jericho Turnpike. (W. Gosden.)

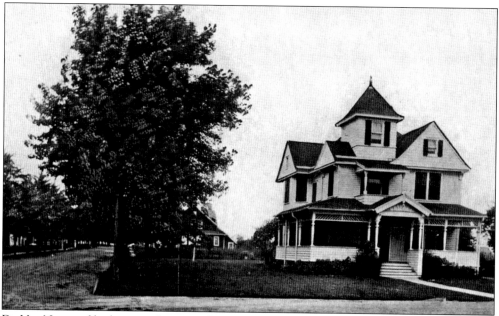

Dr. Van Nostrand had a magnificent residence on Emerson Avenue, fronting onto Lowell Avenue. Van Nostrand was a veterinarian and lived in Floral Park before the village was incorporated. This postcard view dates from about 1900. The northern part of Floral Park village is in the town of North Hempstead, and the area south of Jericho Turnpike is in the town of Hempstead, both part of Nassau County. (FPL.)

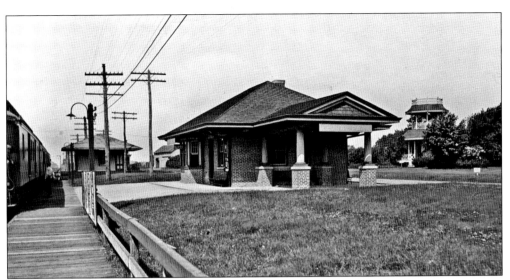

The Floral Park train station, shown above, was built in 1909 and replaced an earlier wood structure that was located north of Tulip Avenue, a short distance away. This masonry building was located between Carnation and Tulip Avenues on the north side of the railroad tracks. This view is looking west, and the Childs's Japanese pagoda can be seen to the right. This was a landmark for train passengers, noting they were in Floral Park. There was also a telegraph office at the station, which was a primary source of communication in the era. The express office, shown below, was a separate building west of the passenger station. Both photographs date from about 1912. The express office was a wood structure used for freight, both receiving and shipping. (Both, FPL.)

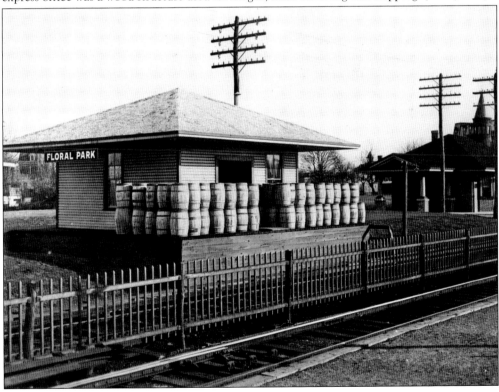

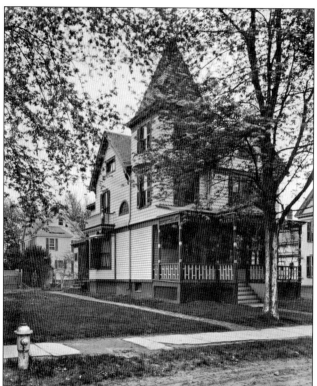

Progress eliminated many early Floral Park homes in the 1960s. Among them was this elegant Victorian home, pictured at left, at the north end of Verbena Avenue. The four early homes there were demolished in November 1960 to make way for an office building. The early residential property was reclassified for commercial use, as the land became more valuable than the structure upon it. (FPL.)

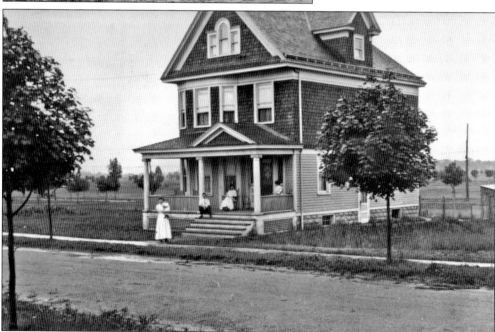

By August 11, 1912, when the photograph above was taken of 58 Aspen Street, the sale of building lots on property that were once fields was well under way. Pictured here is the Brown family, and beyond the house, the streets that had already been cut through can be seen. Paved sidewalks existed, but the roads were still dirt, where ashes from stoves and furnaces were placed. (FPL.)

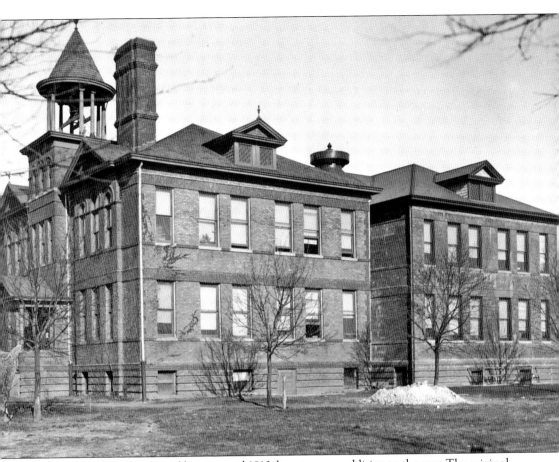

The Floral Park School, pictured here around 1910, boasts a new addition to the rear. The original school was built in 1894 by Mapes and Son to serve the growing population of children in Floral Park. Prior to that date, children had to travel more than 1 mile away to a small wooden, one-room schoolhouse on Jericho Turnpike, in what today is the community of Bellerose Terrace. The Floral Park School faced South Tyson Avenue and was renamed to honor John Lewis Childs in 1929, when an additional elementary school was built in the west end of the village. By the late 1950s, the 1894 and 1910 buildings were deemed too old to upgrade and were demolished, and new structures replaced them. The main entrance then faced Elizabeth Street on the north side of the building. The original school bell in the tower was given to the fire department and is now on the front lawn of the village hall. (FPL.)

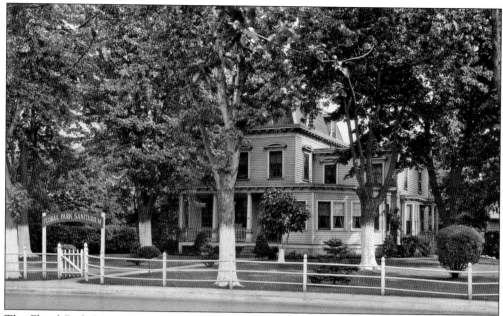

The Floral Park Sanitarium, pictured above in 1927, was located on the south side of Jericho Turnpike in a stately Victorian structure. This was, at one time, a private home, which was converted to a place where people could recover from illness and provide care for mothers in labor, all in a clean, calm, park-like setting. It was the local alternative to traveling to the nearest hospital 5 miles away. (FPL.)

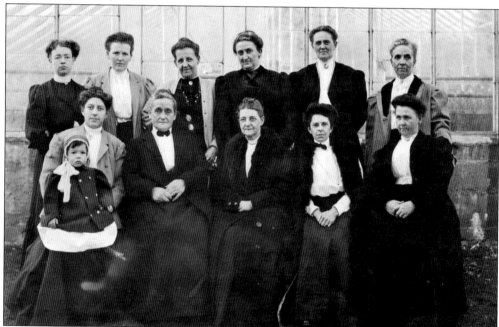

Some early residents pose in front of the Childs greenhouses in this 1908 photograph. From left to right are (seated) Mrs. ? Hansen, Elma Tuthill, Mrs. ? Hendrickson, Mrs. ? Duryea, and Maria Parry; (standing) Mrs. ? Bedell, Mrs. ? Brock, Mrs. ? Fields, Mrs. ? Walker, Mrs. ? Remsen, and Mrs. ? Barto. (FPL.)

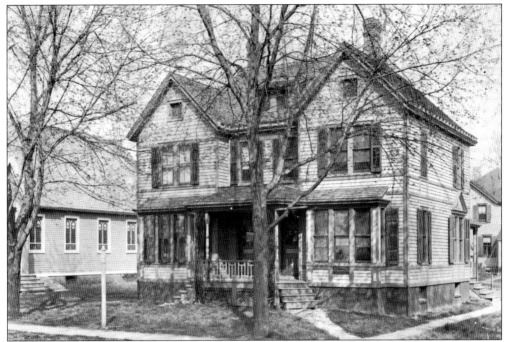

The Wesley Simpson house on Verbena Avenue was built around 1890 and was used as a duplex. The Simpson family occupied the southern half. The northern half, prior to 1904, was used as the parsonage for the Methodist church. The Mansur and Hogan families also resided here at one time as well. Simpson was an electrical contractor, and his business sign was attached to the front of the house. (FPL.)

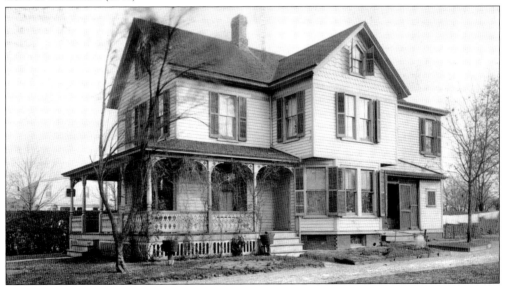

The Ward H. Tilton home, shown above, was the first house on Verbena Avenue, just south of Tulip Avenue. Tilton was the second postmaster of Floral Park from 1894 to 1897. On the left side, looking through the porch, one can make out Childs Hall on Tulip Avenue. By 1906, the house was owned by the Schmensing brothers, who also owned the Park House Hotel at the same time. (FPL.)

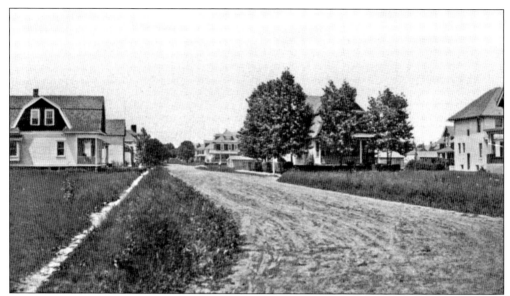

Jacob Oshansky, who ran a candy and novelty store on Jericho Turnpike just a few blocks away, published this postcard view of Elizabeth Street. This area of land was owned by the Spooner family, and Spooner Street is one block north of Elizabeth Street. The House and Home Company developed the area in 1906, and many of the homes built then still remain today. (FPL.)

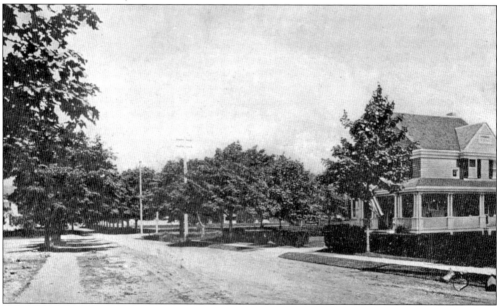

This postcard image is looking northwest on Tulip Avenue toward Plainfield Avenue. The house pictured belonged to the Wright family, who had settled in Floral Park before 1900. Andrew Wright owned the house, shown in 1906, and William A. Wright, who was a charter member of the local Lions Club in 1925, would eventually own it. The house was sold to St. Elizabeth's Church in the early 1950s. (FPL.)

Four

A Village Incorporated

The first decade of the 20th century saw rapid growth in Floral Park. The Childs seed and bulb mail-order business had flourished for over three decades by the time the village was incorporated on October 15, 1908, when Childs was 52 years old. The property he and others owned had become valuable real estate and was being divided up into plots so homes could be built among the street patterns that were being established. A Mrs. Spooner owned property around the Floral Park School and so did the Floral Park Land Company. They sold numerous plots of land south of Jericho Turnpike between South Tyson and Plainfield Avenues. The south side and west end of Floral Park were also starting to be developed.

With the influx of new residents drawn to the area by advertisements in newspapers, many civic-minded citizens decided it was time to incorporate as a village. Meetings were held to discuss the matter, and on September 21, 1908, the people of the Hamlet of Floral Park voted to become a village. A large majority approved of the proposal, and paperwork was filed with the state, which was approved on that level in October. At the fire department hall on Violet Avenue, elections were held, and John Lewis Childs was elected the first village president. Four other prominent citizens and local businessmen were also elected to fill the office of trustee: George W. Downing and John F. Klein, with David W. Syme, village clerk, and Andrew Wright, tax collector.

Commercial buildings started to appear along both sides of Jericho Turnpike, and a large controversy, with much heated conversation, ensued when sidewalks started to be laid in 1911 on Tyson Avenue. Coal was the primary fuel source for heating and cooking, and the ash from this was disposed of at the path where the new sidewalks would now line. Many residents did not agree this change was a positive one, as they would have to find a new place to dispose of the ash.

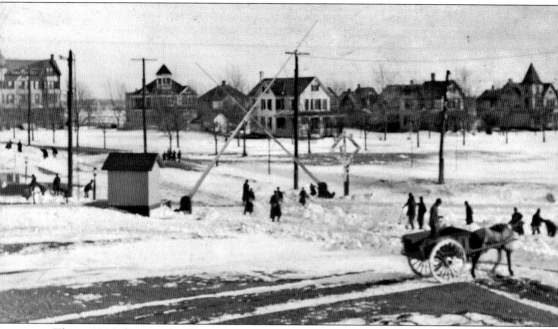

This *c.* 1905 photograph of snow removal, by shovel, at the Tulip Avenue gate crossing was taken from the second story of the Childs seed house looking southwest. The Park House Hotel, built by John Lewis Childs to accommodate visitors to the area, as well as give employees a place to live, is located in the rear left of the photograph. To the immediate right of that is the firehouse, which, in a few years, would also serve as the first village hall when Floral Park became incorporated in 1908. Both of these structures were on Violet Avenue. The houses seen to the right are on Verbena Avenue, one block farther north. Telegraph poles can be seen in the area closest to the railroad track. The small shed next to the gate crossing was a shelter for the man who hand-cranked the mechanism to raise and lower the gates, as required. (FPL.)

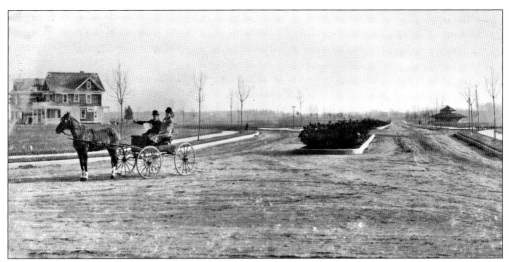

In this view of Floral Parkway, the building at right in the distance was a real estate office. When this image was taken around 1908, the farmland southeast from the corner of Tulip and Plainfield Avenues had just been divided into building lots, and a street pattern was laid out. The islands in the center of the road are unique to this particular area. (VFP.)

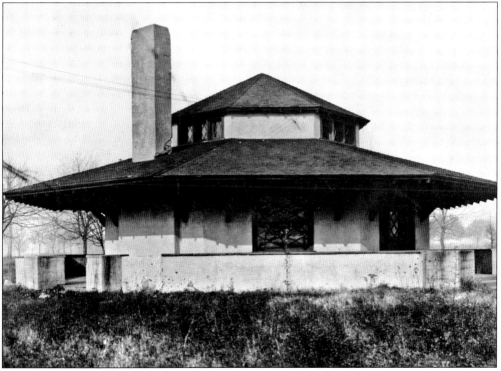

The Round House, at the corner of Floral Parkway and Carnation Avenue, was named because of its six sides. The photograph dates from 1908 and the building from 1905. It was the office of McCormack Real Estate and the Windsor Land Company. Eventually it would be added on to and later served as a meeting hall, a private home, and, for many years, as a church. (FPL.)

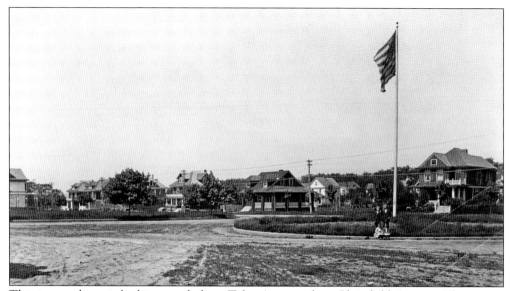

This image above is looking south from Tulip Avenue along Plainfield Avenue. The year is approximately 1920, and the circle with the flagpole is the Veterans Memorial Park, which was just starting to be developed. This area in the 1860s and 1880s was known as Plainfield and was joined on its northwest border by East Hinsdale. (FPL.)

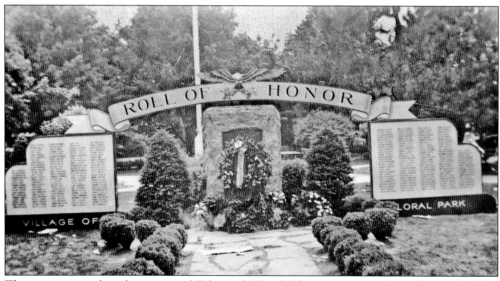

The war memorial at the corner of Tulip and Plainfield Avenues is in the village park. This photograph was taken soon after the roll of honor, listing the names of Floral Park residents who served in the armed forces, was constructed to recognize their devotion to their country. This area has been revamped and enhanced over the decades as a permanent place of honor. (FPL.)

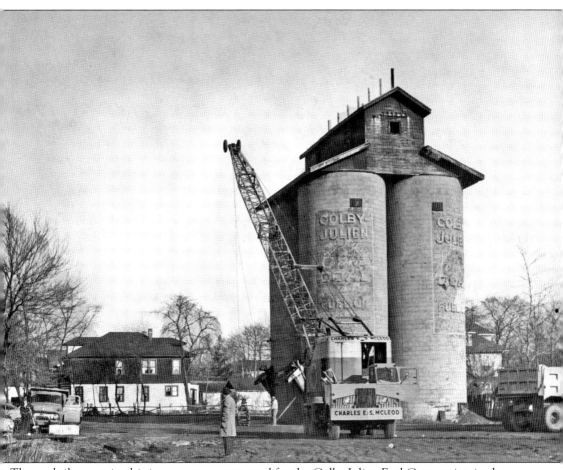

The coal silos seen in this image were constructed for the Colby-Julien Fuel Corporation in the 1920s on the south side of the Creedmoor Branch of the Long Island Railroad. Coal was the primary source of heat and cooking fuel for decades in Floral Park, and Colby-Julien was one of a trio of companies within the borders of the village that had these huge masonry storage silos. All were located near railroad tracks for easy access to coal railcars. These particular silos were demolished in January 1959. The sole remaining group of coal silos still standing in the village to this day are a few blocks away from those shown here. The cost to demolish them safely became too great for the owners of the property, so the alternative use now has been to use them as cell phone receiver towers. (VFP.)

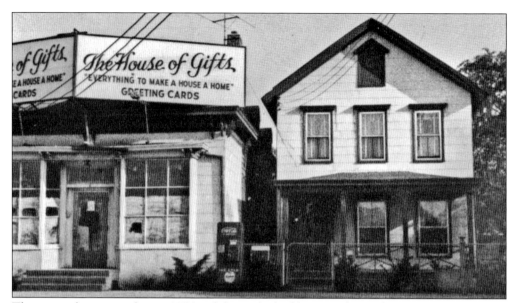

The image above was taken in 1956 and shows the buildings on the southwest corner of Remsen Lane and Jericho Turnpike. Both structures dated from the early 1870s and, before 1900, were owned by Edward L. Frost. By 1906, they were part of the Hallock property. A general store was located in the building at left, as was the Hinsdale post office. (VFP.)

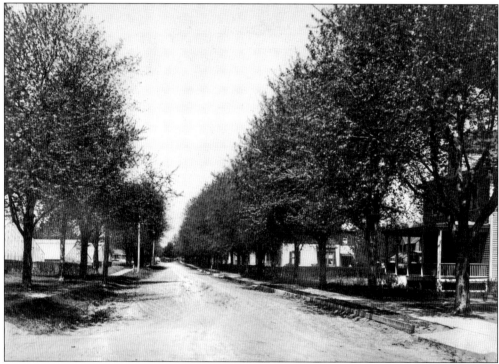

This photograph of Verbena Avenue, just north of Carnation Avenue, shows the greenhouses of Charles H. Allen at left. Roads in Floral Park were still dirt when this image was taken, around 1912. Telephone poles were just starting to appear, and curbs near the paved sidewalks were made of wood and were installed by the owner of the property. (VFP.)

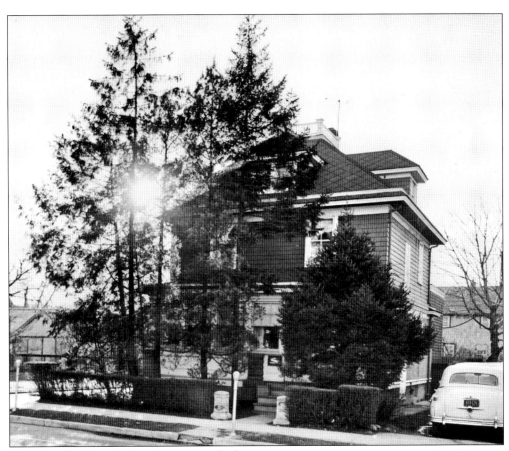

The Krug family settled in this area just before the Civil War and had farmland near Tulip and Covert Avenues. The house shown above belonged to Stephen Krug and was located on South Tyson Avenue. It was built in 1913 and was demolished in 1958 to make way for the new Floral Park Savings and Loan Association building. Krug was the contractor who built Our Lady of Victory Church. (FPV.)

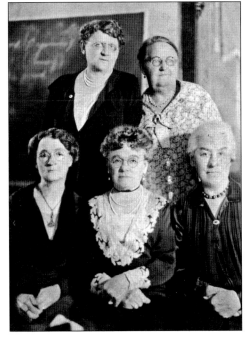

A group of prominent Floral Park ladies is shown in this undated photograph at right. From left to right are (seated) Mrs. Willett Bedell, Mrs. Edward L. Frost, and Mrs. William N. Bird; (standing) Mrs. Jessie Freestone and Mrs. Frank Field. The husbands of these ladies were all prominent citizens who were heavily involved in a variety of civic matters, ranging from the fire department, court system, and athletic organizations to church activities. (VFP.)

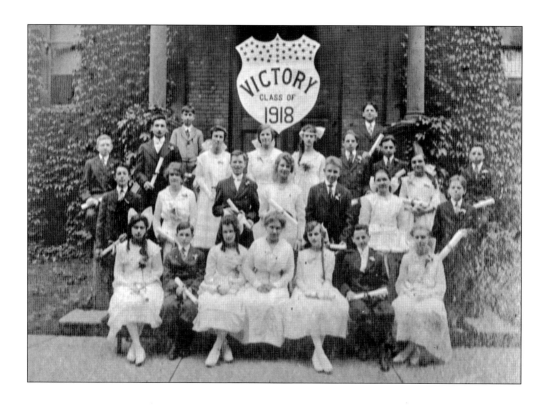

In the above photograph, the eighth-grade graduating class, shown on the front steps of the Floral Park School, was called the "Victory Class of 1918." They celebrated the end of the Great War in Europe, later known as World War I. To attend high school they would have to travel to Jamaica, Queens, or Hempstead High School, as there was no local high schools until 1930. The image of the auditorium below shows the additions that were made to the school in 1920. The auditorium faced south toward the nearby railroad tracks. At the extreme left, the cone-shaped bell tower at the front of the school is visible. (Both, FPL.)

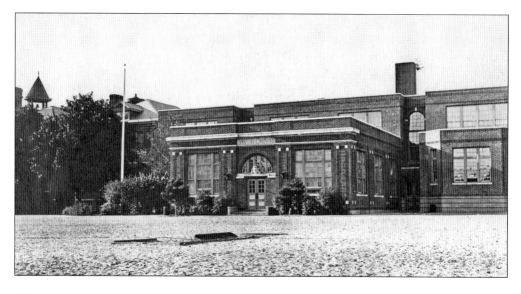

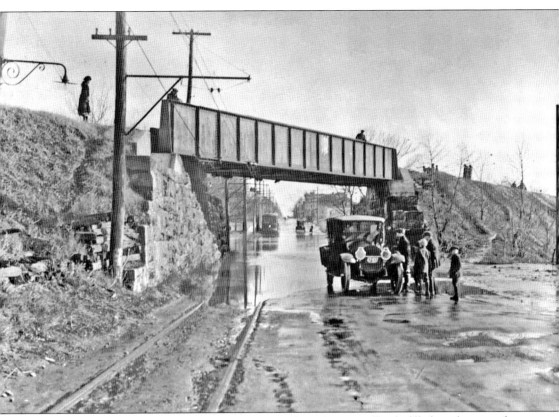

This view is of Jericho Turnpike looking east around 1915. Spring floods filled roadways with water, even on main state roads like this. The new Locomobile chauffeur-driven town car has its hood up after it stalled going through deep water. Local children observe the scene from the road, as well as from the iron bridge above that was for the Creedmoor Spur of the Long Island Railroad. The trolley tracks of the New York and Long Island Traction Company can be seen in the foreground and a trolley in the distance. This bridge was enlarged twice before the spur was abandoned, and the bridge was removed in 1975. Trolley service ceased in 1926 as bus service increased, as did the use of private passenger car use. The poles along the road carried electric power, which, in this era, was just becoming popular in use. Telephone service in Floral Park at this time was minimal. (VFP.)

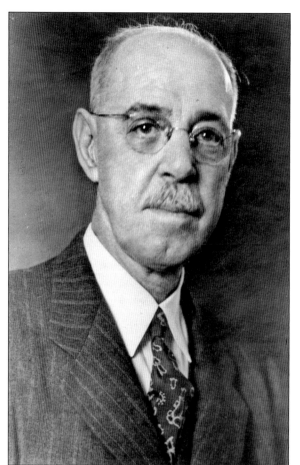

The Heidtmann family has been in Floral Park for decades. Frederick H. Heidtmann, shown in the photograph at left, was mayor of the village from 1939 to 1947 and trustee from 1935 to 1939. The Heidtmanns were builder-contractors and constructed the corner store for John Lewis Childs. (VFP.)

By 1912, business buildings besides those owned by John Lewis Childs were beginning to be established on Tulip Avenue, just east of the railroad tracks. Below, at left is the Howard James Hardware Store that offered a good variety of household furnishings. The center store was an ice-cream parlor and grocery store, and Childs Hall served as a meeting place and an office for the Flowerfield Reality Company and George Hurrell's Construction Company. (FPL.)

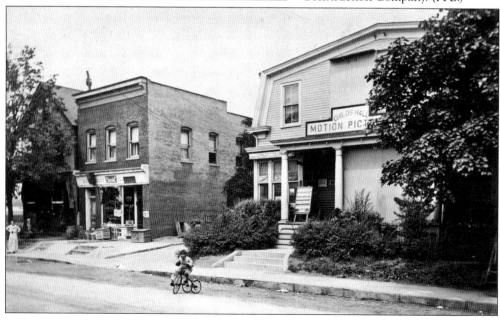

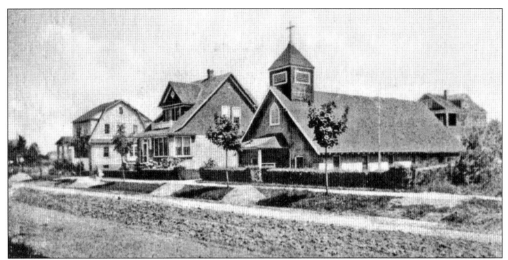

The Lutheran church, as viewed in the postcard above, was built on Holland Avenue in 1914–1915. The congregation was incorporated in November 1913 as the Christ Evangelical Lutheran Church of Floral Park. When a new building was erected on Spooner Street in 1925, this building was sold, and in 1960, it was occupied by the Veterans of Foreign Wars. (FPL.)

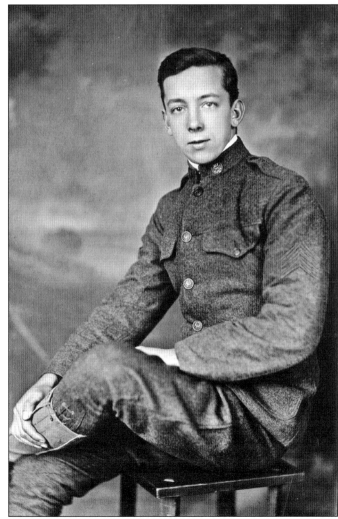

Byron Thurston sits for the portrait shown at right before he left for service in World War I. He was one of three men from Floral Park that died in that war; the other two were Mortimer Lyons and Harry Homeyer. The Thurston family lived on Magnolia Avenue, and Byron's father, Wallace Thurston, was postmaster of Floral Park from 1924 to 1932. (FPV.)

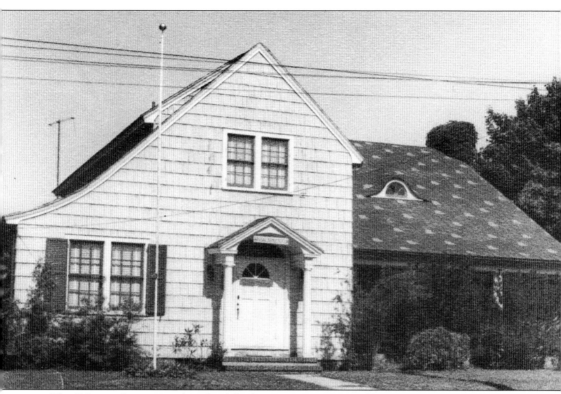

The "Nassaus" was started in the fall of 1910. It was organized by a group of baseball enthusiasts who wanted to keep in touch over the winter months. Until 1913, only the 10 original members gathered and paid dues of 10¢ per week, after the initial fee of $1. The name was changed to the Nassau Athletic Club in 1914, and membership was opened to other men in the community. It was incorporated in 1923, and basketball replaced baseball as the favored sport, due to lack of playing space for the latter. By 1928, the building seen above was erected on the west side of Plainfield Avenue, just north of the Belmont racetrack. This new facility had a large meeting room, showers, and a kitchen, as well as other amenities. Large tennis courts were located at the rear of the property and became the predominant athletic activity. Many social events were held here by groups that rented the building for the next 70-plus years. (VFP.)

The Oshansky family moved to Floral Park in 1911, and Jacob Oshansky built this store at 161 Jericho Turnpike in 1917. The photograph at right dates from the 1920s, when Louis Oshansky, Jacob's son, managed the store. The family also built a stationary store on Tulip Avenue, which was run by brother and sister Harry and Ester Oshansky. (FPL.)

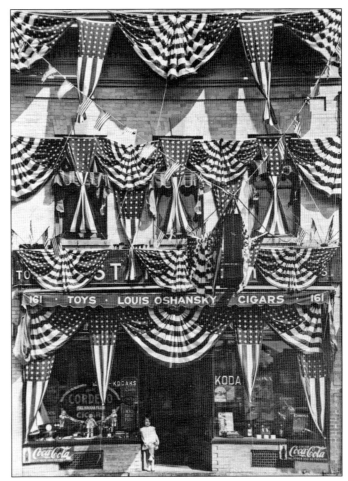

The business section along the north side of Jericho Turnpike had filled in by the early 1920s. The National Bank and Trust Company replaced the building David Syme had constructed there earlier on the corner of Hindsdale Avenue. This building would remain a bank building, with different savings and loan companies. By the 1950s, Franklin National Bank was located there, but the structure was torn down in 1960. (FPL.)

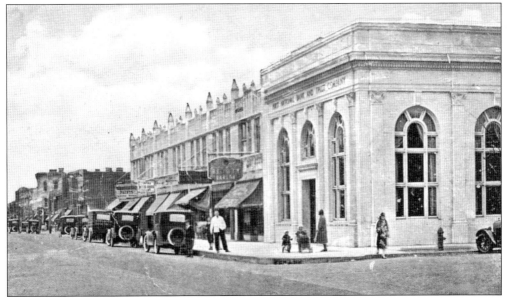

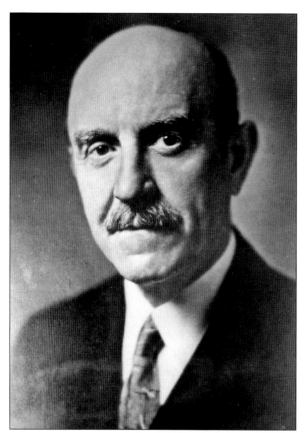

John McNeil, shown in the photograph at left, was a major builder and businessman in Floral Park in the 1920s and 1930s. His company built the Floral Theatre, and when completed, his holding corporation also operated the theater. His construction company also built the Floral Park–Bellerose School in 1928. McNeil was also active in civic matters and government. He served as a village trustee in 1927–1929 and as village mayor from 1929 to 1939. (VFP.)

The photograph below, taken before 1900, shows a house located on the south side of Carnation Avenue on either the Sibley or Chisholm property. There were several farmhouses on these properties, which joined at the north property line. The Sibley property, which faced Floral Boulevard, was eventually sold; the houses were demolished, and the site became a lumberyard in the 1920s. (FPL.)

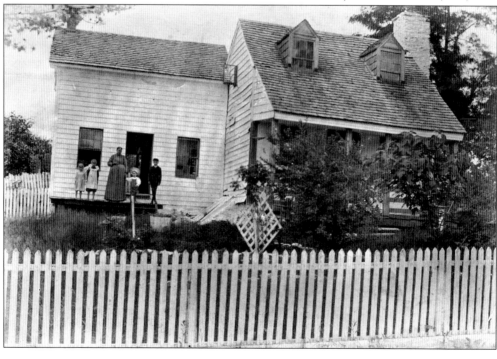

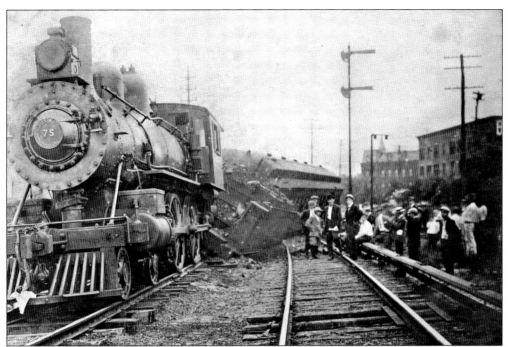

The wreck of the Long Island Railroad steam train No. 75 took place on September 8, 1912. It was an express train on its way to Lake Ronkonkoma in Suffolk County. The train was due in Mineola, New York, at 5:00 p.m., but soon after the last car cleared Tulip Avenue, the train derailed. The train was reported at the time as traveling 50 miles per hour, and it was suspected that perhaps a switch was left open that allowed the steam engine to cross over onto the electric rail, which ran parallel to the main line at that point. The tender and smoking car overturned, but the two following cars remained upright on the main line. There were no injuries from the accident. At right in the background of the above photograph are the Tyson Building and the Childs seed house. (Both, FPL.)

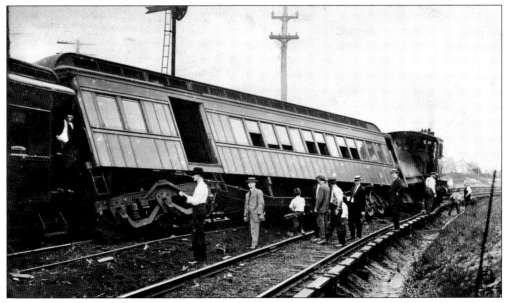

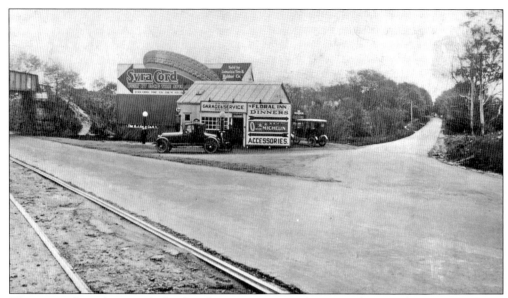

This image shows how rural Floral Park was in 1919. Jericho Turnpike is in the foreground, and Tulip Avenue is on the right. The trolley tracks seen at the bottom of the photograph remained until 1926. The railroad bridge at left is the Creedmoor Spur. The Floral Inn mentioned on the sign is the former Childs Park House Hotel and was advertising its chicken, duck, and squab dinners. (FPL.)

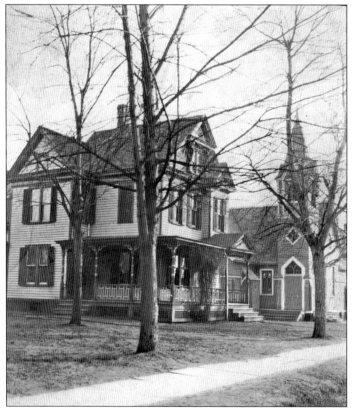

R. V. Constable owned this home, which was located just north of the Methodist church on Verbena Avenue. His property extended back to the west to Violet Avenue. By the 1950s, this property was zoned for commercial development, and this house, as well as two others, were demolished to make way for an office building and parking lot. (FPL.)

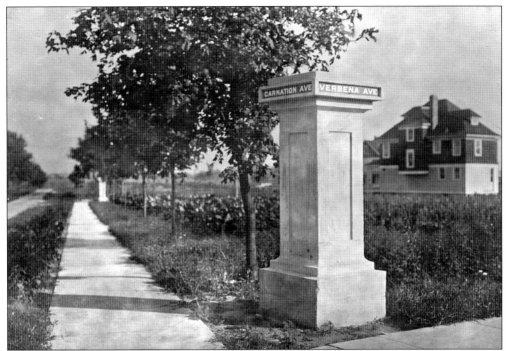

This early street sign is pictured at the corner of Carnation and Verbena Avenues looking west toward Violet Avenue. Sidewalks were installed, but the road was still unpaved dirt. The street marker was made of concrete, as was the one on the next corner, which can be seen in the distance. Few houses existed south of Carnation Avenue around 1913, when this photograph was taken. (FPL.)

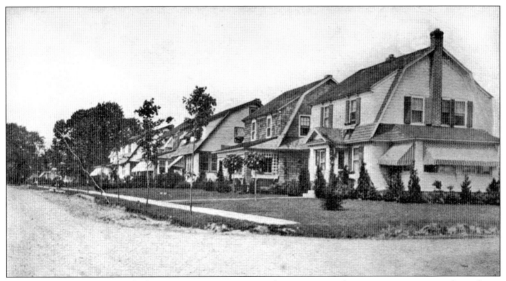

Remsen Lane was named after George B. Remsen, who was an early property owner and resident. He was active in the formation of Hook and Ladder Company No. 1 in 1893. This postcard image shows the street as it appeared about 1925. Remsen Lane is the west border that separates the Villages of Floral Park and Bellerose. It remains much the same today as viewed here. (FPL.)

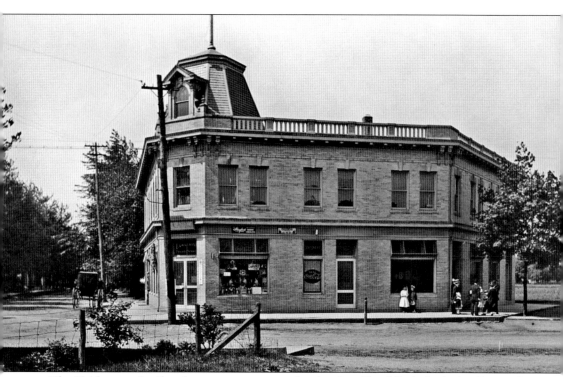

The Heidtmann family, who were contractors that lived in Floral Park, built the Corner Store for John Lewis Childs. The post office relocated to this building, and the Heidtmanns had their offices on the second floor. This view shows the building as it faced Tulip Avenue looking west, with Verbena Avenue at left. With Belmont Park just 1 mile south of the village, the Corner Store stocked many items that the equine population at the track required, and next to the cigars and candy in the store were large quantities of lineament, blankets, and saddle soap. The first proprietors of the store were Johnson and Childs, and soon after, the Ullman family took over the business. By 1917, the general store had also become a pharmacy, and a Mr. O'Toole operated it from 1917 to 1921, when it was taken over by Clinton Ramee, who operated it from 1921 until 1956. Its final owner was Frank Vita, who operated it until the building was torn down in 1960. (FPL.)

Five

JAZZ AGE AND THE GREAT DEPRESSION

The post–World War I era saw the village expand its services to meet the needs of the ever-growing population. The first uniformed police officers were hired, and a small police booth was built after the armistice near Jericho Turnpike and South Tyson Avenue. The fire department expanded with the construction of two new firehouses. The Reliance Engine Company had a one-story masonry building constructed on Spooner Street in 1917, just west of Plainfield Avenue, and the Active Hose and Engine Company was formed, with a firehouse built on Atlantic Avenue in 1924. Three firehouses in one village might seem excessive, but the railroad running through the center of the village stopped all north and south travel when a train went through. Fires did not wait to be extinguished because a passing train blocked firefighters.

In 1929, most of the wood-frame structures located on Tulip Avenue that were 40 years old or more were demolished, and masonry buildings were erected in their place. The same was true along Jericho Turnpike. New schools, built in 1929, included the Floral Park–Bellerose School in the west end and Sewanhaka High School, which opened in 1930 at the southwest corner of the village. Built in 1935, a new village hall housed a new firehouse at one end and a library area at the opposite end.

Located on Jericho Turnpike, only one block apart from each other, the Lily and Floral Theatres dominated entertainment. The latest silent and, later talking, pictures were shown, in addition to regular performances of vaudeville acts. Houses and stores built on the land wiped out almost all traces of the former seed and florist businesses. Floral Park's founder died in 1921, but his widow remained at the family home until her demise in 1937.

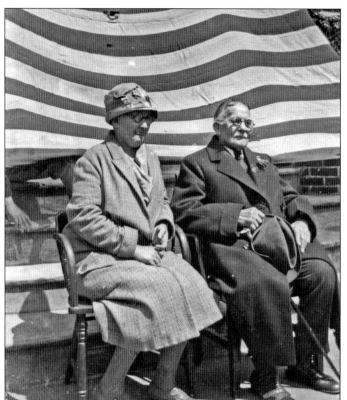

Raymond and Jean Stokley are pictured at left in May 1929 at a John Lewis Childs School ceremony. Stokley was the last veteran of the Civil War who resided in Floral Park. On occasion, he would speak to the children at the school of his experiences in the war. He died five years later, at the age of 91. (FPL.)

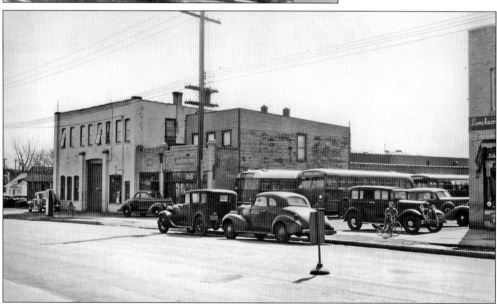

The above image dates from 1939 and shows the Schenck Transportation Company at 368–372 Jericho Turnpike. Howard Schenck's bus service was a large operation during the era when independent owners operated routes in Nassau County. Schenck used Mack buses almost exclusively for school and commuter transportation, and he ran a viable business before the Metropolitan Suburban Bus Authority (MSBA) took control in 1973. (VFP.)

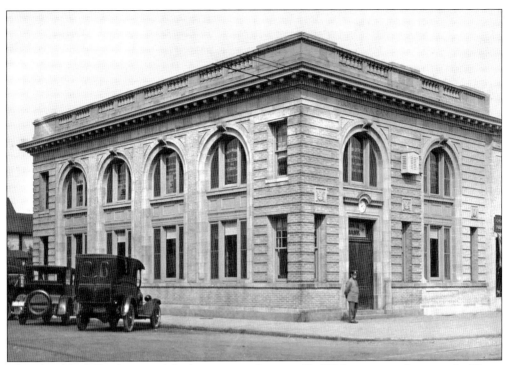

The Floral Park Bank opened for business on January 27, 1908, in a storefront in the Tyson Building. In 1918, it moved to a new building on the north side of Jericho Turnpike. A decade later, when these images date from, the bank had to expand again, and the occasion of the expansion is depicted in the group photograph below. The bank president, Edward L. Frost, is shown at center with a trowel in his hand. The chief cashier of the bank was Charles H. Van Nostrand, and he is the first man on the right in the first row. The bank building was a fixture on Jericho Turnpike. The bank building was converted to the Scher Furniture store and was later demolished in 1960. (Both, FPL.)

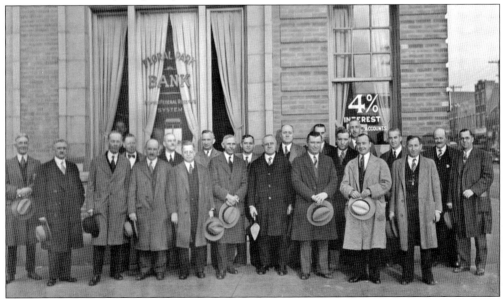

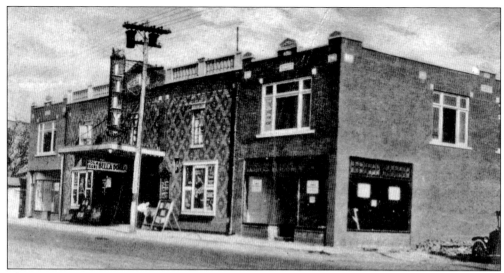

The Lily Theatre was the first major motion picture and vaudeville theater in Floral Park. It was on Jericho Turnpike next to Flower Avenue. The building was erected soon after World War I. This postcard dates from 1924, when the buildings on either side of it had just been built. In 1950, the building was reworked to accommodate a Firestone Tire Store, which continues to this day. (FPL.)

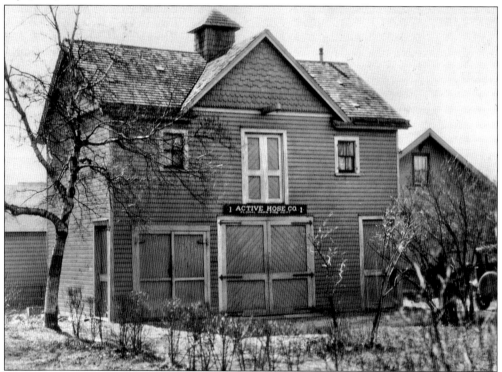

When the Active Hose and Engine Company formed on March 20, 1924, it was located at the very west end of the village. This photograph from 1927 shows the barn behind the Victorian house on the corner of Crocus and Chestnut Avenues that was used as a firehouse until a two-story brick structure on Atlantic Avenue was built by the village as a permanent home. (VFP.)

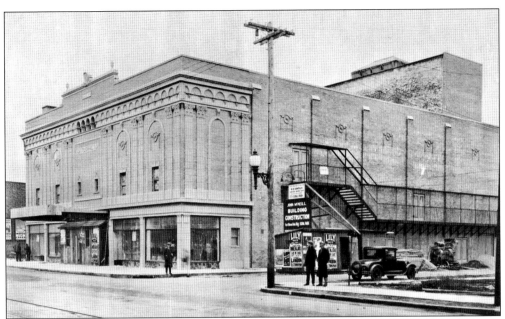

The Floral Theatre is shown nearing completion in February 1927 in the photograph above. John McNeill's construction company not only built this elaborate movie palace, but his Holding Company also owned it. By the time the Floral Theatre was completely finished, McNeill was on his way to being elected mayor of Floral Park. The Floral Theatre was equipped to show the latest talking pictures, but it also played host to vaudeville acts, which, as a form of entertainment, were soon to meet their demise. The postcard image below shows the completed theater with its huge marquee. It remained exactly the same until the state widened Jericho Turnpike in 1960, and the original marquee had to be removed because it hung out too far over the road. When the theater closed 70 years later, it converted to an upscale banquet facility. (Both, FPHS.)

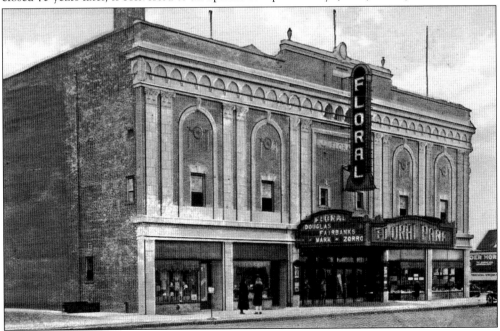

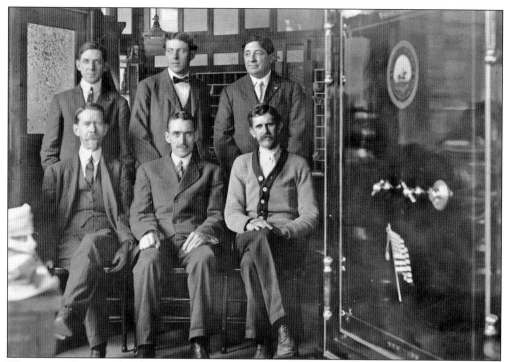

These two photographs show employees of the Floral Park Post Office. The late-1890s image above was taken in the building on South Tyson Avenue. From left to right are (seated) Wallace Thurston; Walter Neil Pike, who was postmaster from 1907 to 1914; and John Van Nostrand; (standing) Harry McNutley, George Downing, and Garrett Duryea. The image below was taken on April 29, 1932, when the post office relocated to the Knights of Columbus building. By 1932, the post office had a small, motorized fleet of vehicles used to transport and deliver mail. Standing at far left is Joseph Mara, who became postmaster in 1933 and held that position until 1955, and fourth from left is Wallace Thurston. (Both, VFP.)

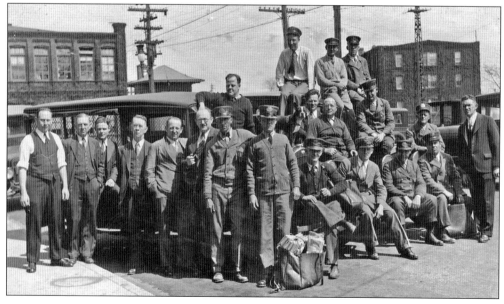

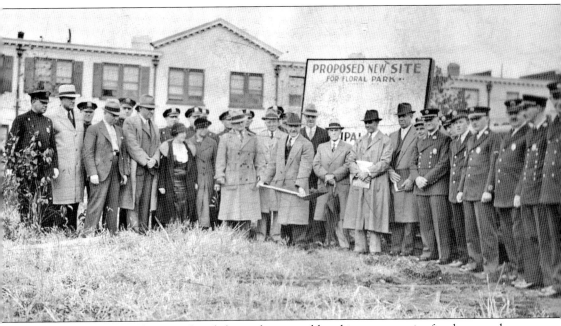

This photograph dates from 1935 and shows the ground-breaking ceremonies for the area the new village hall would be built on. It was located at the start of Floral Boulevard on land that was originally owned by John Lewis Childs and was used as a baseball field. Vernon and Carlton Streets, which were named for John Lewis Childs's sons, flank the property. Mayor John McNeil is shown at center with the spade in his hands. Among those pictured with the mayor are police officer Bill Pfeiffer, police chief James Humphry, officer Joe Knight, trustee Gilbert Dingley, trustee E. Stanley Bosanko, village clerk John Blome, trustee Fred Heidtmann, village historian Howard James, George Rettinger, and Arthur Ennis. The new masonry building would replace the wood-frame building located one block east on Violet Avenue that had been built in 1901 as the firehouse and meeting hall. The new building was completed and opened by 1936 and still serves its purpose to this day. (VFP.)

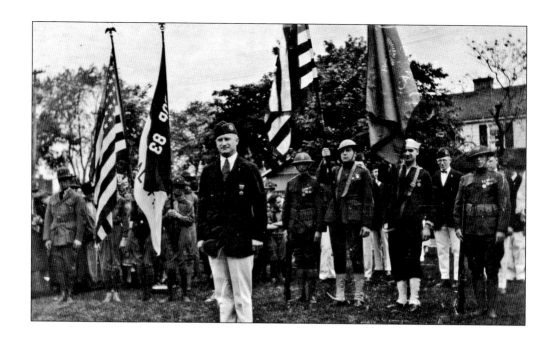

The annual Memorial Day observance and ceremonies have always been a Floral Park tradition. The Floral Park Post No. 334 of the American Legion was organized in August 1919, and the photograph shows the event around 1925. At center is E. Stanley Bosanko, the post commander, while behind him is color bearer Howard Ballison, and Phillip Pellegrino holds the legion banner. Stanley Bosanko helped form the Citizens Party, a local political group in 1928, and from 1932 to 1936, he was a trustee of the village, as well as acting mayor. A group of veterans of foreign wars also participated, but they did not organize to form a post until 1939. At right in the photograph below is Wesley B. Simpson, who organized the post and become its first commander. (Both, VFP.)

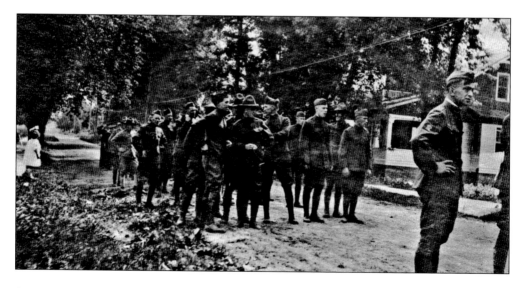

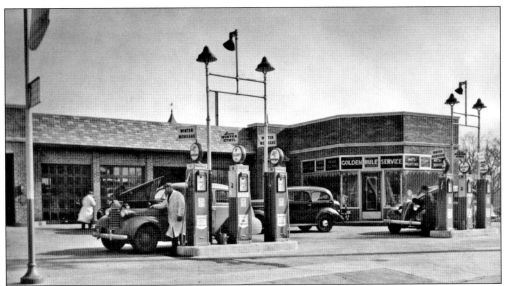

This 1937 photograph shows the Golden Rule Service Station on Carnation Avenue at Atlantic Avenue. Benjamin "Bennie" Dubin and his partner, Considine, owned the Mobilgas-Socony Station. It was a fairly new station when this image was taken. Dubin can be seen looking into the motor of the Oldsmobile at center. Today the scene remains much the same as it did then. (VFP.)

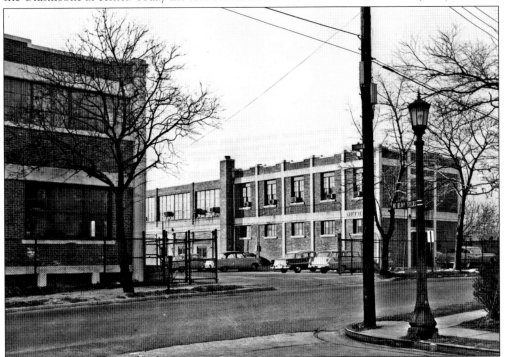

Warehouse and storage areas in Floral Park are rare. The one large cluster of buildings is on Carnation Avenue adjacent to the railroad tracks. Prior to 1900, this property was the site of an early tavern, and later buildings provided housing for the employees of John Lewis Childs, who owned the property. This 1957 photograph shows the current buildings that were erected in the 1920s. (VFP.)

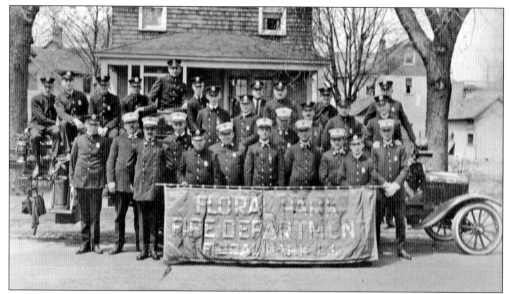

The Floral Park Hook and Ladder Company No. 1 formed in May 1893. By 1923, the Village of Floral Park appropriated funds for a new motorized Ford fire engine. Shown in the above photograph are the volunteer firefighters, posing with their new truck. As years progressed and population increased, the Alert Engine Company (1907), the Reliance Engine Company (1910), the Active Hose and Engine Company (1924), and the Rescure Company (1930) were added. (VFP.)

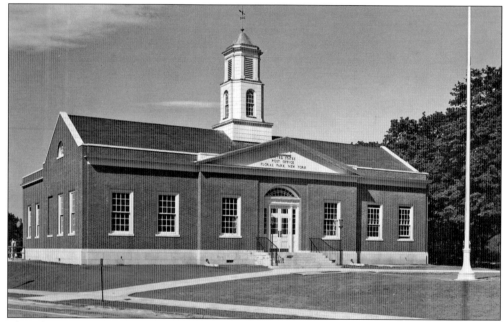

This photograph shows the new Floral Park Post Office just as it was being completed in 1936. It was built on property once owned by John Lewis Childs, who lived across the street in his mansion. The building faces east, looking at the railroad crossing at Tulip Avenue. By 1963, the facility became too small to house the post office. It became the library in 1964, when the village acquired the site and building. (VFP.)

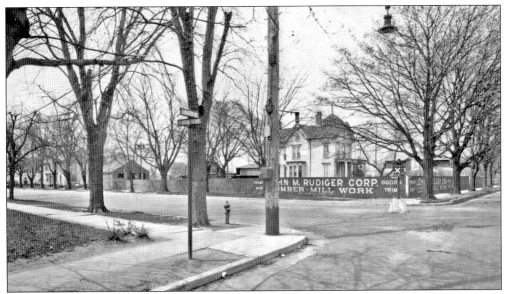

The John M. Rudiger Corporation—a supplier of lumber, doors, and trim, and a provider of millwork—established its business at the corner of Floral Boulevard and Carnation Avenue soon after World War I. The business was successful for a number of years, despite competition from the larger lumberyard of Henry W. Burt, who also carried masonry supplies, on Jericho Turnpike. The image above shows the Rudiger Corporation at its peak. It is shown below after a huge fire around 1927. Vehicles, machinery, and lumber were lost in the fire, which was difficult to control due to the enormous amount of wood the fire could feed on. The business was deemed a total loss, and in 1939, luxury garden apartments were built on the site, which remain to this day. (Both, VFP.)

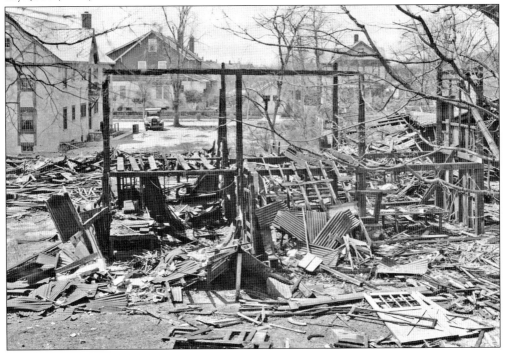

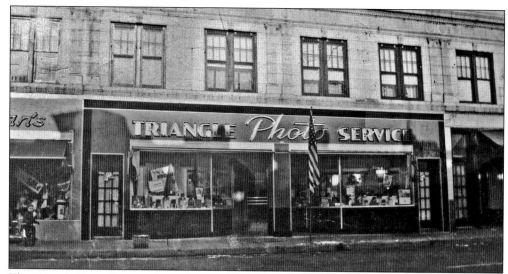

The Triangle Photo Service, shown here in the 1940s, was located at 125 Tulip Avenue. William C. Jagy was the owner of this business, which started prior to World War II. The shop processed and printed rolls of film that were dropped off at hundreds of pharmacies all over Long Island. Ann Ault was the counter person there for many years. (Carson family.)

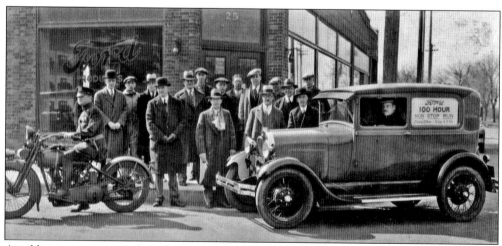

A publicity stunt to introduce the new Ford in the autumn of 1928 was held under the watchful eye of the police department. Posed in front of the Ford dealership at 25 Atlantic Avenue is a new Ford sedan, ready for its "100 hour nonstop run" from Monday at 12:00 p.m. to Friday at 4:00 p.m. David Herk is the police officer on the motorcycle. (VFP.)

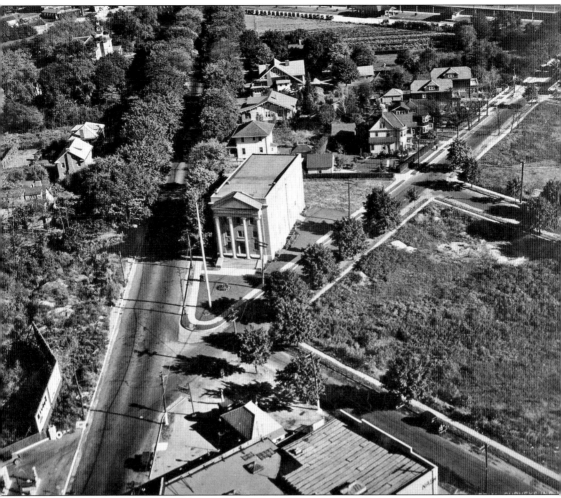

This aerial view of the fork in the road shows where Tulip Avenue (left) is joined by Carnation Avenue (right). The Masonic Temple at the center, with its large columns, has been a landmark in Floral Park since it was built in 1925. It became an instant recognizable symbol when entering the village from the northwest. The large empty lots at right in this view had houses built there in the late 1930s, and in the postwar era, two-story garden apartments developed along the west edge of Carnation Avenue. The Childs mansion can be seen at the top left corner of the photograph, and his house, along with the other two houses on that side of Tulip Avenue, were demolished in the postwar era to build garden apartment houses and a post office. (FPL.)

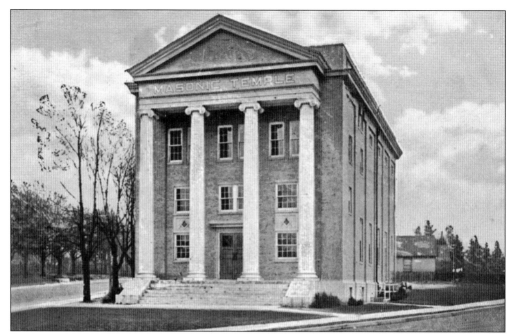

By the mid-1920s, many organizations started to form in the community, and one of the most active was the Masons. It was an era of fund-raising and the construction of magnificent buildings in classic styles. The building served the Masons long and well, and many village parties were held here by various groups who rented the hall from the Masons. (W. Gosden.)

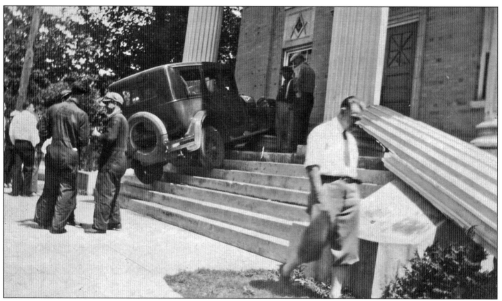

This photograph shows Harry Tooker's Hudson sedan on the steps of the Masonic Temple. He lost control of his car on July 19, 1929, after push-starting it down the hill at Little Neck Parkway. Once started, it took off across Jericho Turnpike and wound up climbing the steps and destroying one of the wood columns at the front of the hall, where it came to rest at the top of the stairs. (FPHS.)

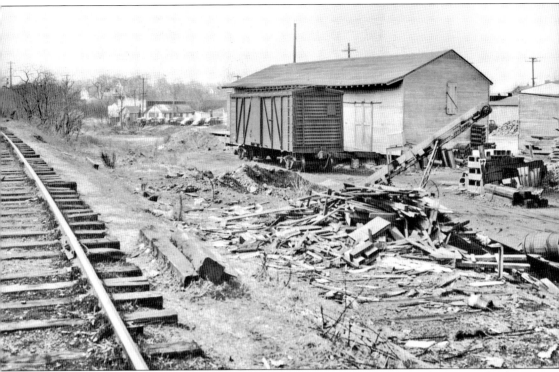

The Creedmoor spur rail line was created in 1871 as part of the Central Railroad of Long Island by the founder of Garden City, Alexander Stewart. This line was first leased, then eventually purchased by the Long Island Railroad in 1892. By 1939, the date of this photograph, the line was seldom used and then only by freight cars. There was a grade-level crossing at South Tyson Avenue immediately south of the John Lewis Childs School with no gate, and the big black iron bridge spanned Jericho Turnpike at its northwest end as it left the village. As can be seen in this photograph, heavy industrial areas backed up to the tracks, and the area became loaded with debris and was a breeding ground for vermin. By the early 1980s, the village was in negotiations with the railroad, and in a successful outcome, the village reworked the property into a much-needed parking lot. (VFP.)

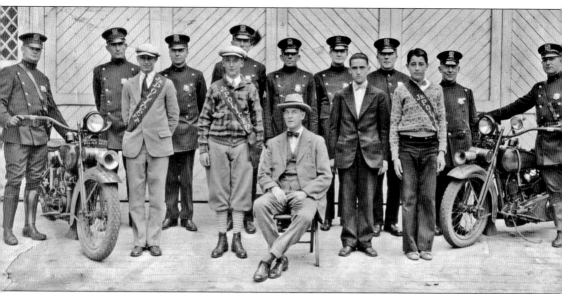

Police chief Robert Ferris is seated at the center in this photograph, taken around 1930. The Junior Police boys are not identified, but the full-time officers are, from left to right, David Herk, John Skinder, Arthur Stubenvoll, James Humphrey, James Pederson, Frank Carlough Sr., Frederik Humphrey, James Toner, and George Considine. Law enforcement officers were first appointed in 1908, when the village was formed, and were called deputy sheriffs. A decade later saw the first organized police in uniform. A small police booth was constructed on South Tyson Avenue for shelter and headquarters, as most police presence was required near Jericho Turnpike, which was the most actively traveled road. A used Harley Davidson motorcycle was purchased for motorized pursuit, as needed, in the mid-1920s, to be followed by a used Ford roadster, and then finally a new Chevrolet patrol car. The police department finally had permanent headquarters at the newly constructed village hall in 1936. (VFP.)

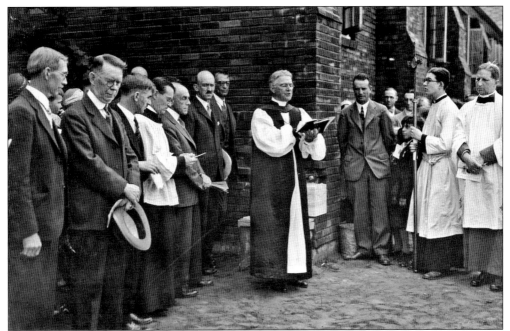

On June 3, 1928, the cornerstone for the new St. Elizabeth's Church was installed during a ceremony at the Harvard Street location. Like other churches in Floral Park, St. Elizabeth's held services in several buildings and locations before this building was constructed. The building replaced a 1918 wood structure located a block away. (FPL.)

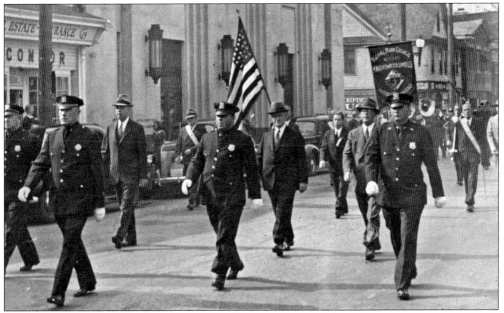

Pictured here is the 1939 Veterans Day parade looking west on Jericho Turnpike at the corner of South Tyson Avenue. Leading the parade was police chief James Humphrey, who is second from left, and immediately behind him is Mayor Fred Heidtmann. The Knights of Columbus received their charter in February 1922. The art deco bank building in the background, built in 1929, replaced Richter's Hotel. (VFP.)

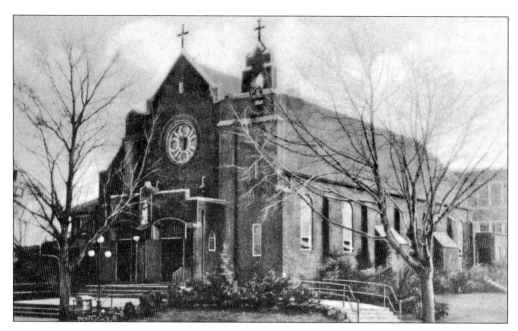

Our Lady of Victory Catholic Church was established to provide religious services for the English-speaking Catholics in the village. Mass was held at the fire department hall on Violet Avenue and then at Childs Hall on Tulip Avenue until 1924. The Krug Construction Company built the church at Plainfield Avenue, Floral Parkway, and Bellmore Street, which was completed in 1924. The Parish School and convent were built on property south of the church in 1930. This property was once a farm, and the early farmhouse was demolished to make way for this structure. It is an active church and school, and the auditorium and cafeteria area in the school have been used for many events by organizations in the village. The church pictured above and the school shown below still appear virtually the same as they did 80 years ago. (Both, FPL.)

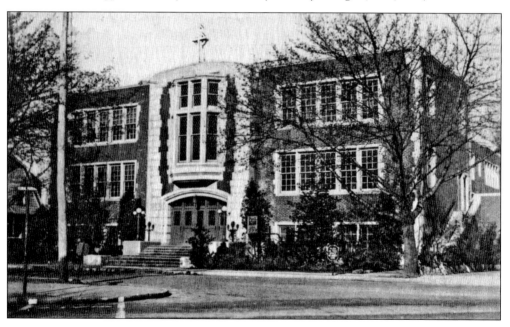

Alan Dinehart was an actor and playwright who was well known in the 1920s and 1930s. He started to act in motion pictures in 1931 and worked for Universal and Columbia Studios. He and his family lived in Floral Park for some time at 339 Tulip Avenue. This image dates from 1933, when he was active as a character and supporting actor. (W. Gosden.)

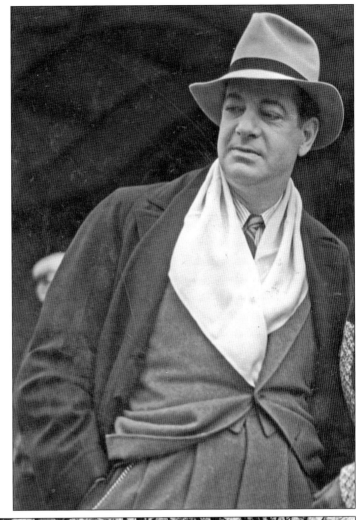

During a severe snow storm in 1934, when the photograph below was taken, tractors were used to move snow, as trucks with plows were not used by the village during this era. The road being cleared is Verbena Avenue, just north of Carnation Avenue. The George Hurrell home is on the corner, and the Methodist church parsonage is located directly behind the tractor. (VFP.)

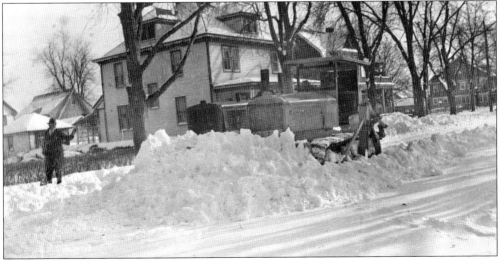

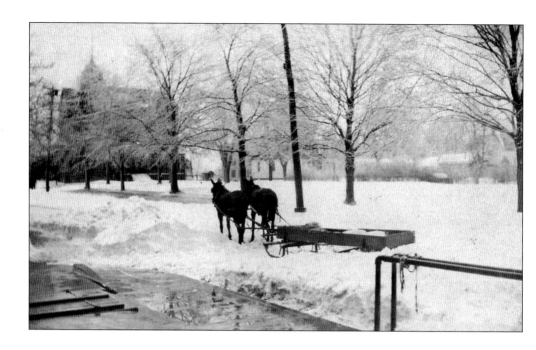

These two winter scenes are of Tulip Avenue east of the railroad tracks. Tulip Avenue was formally known as the Light Horse Road in the mid-19th century and was renamed after Childs arrived. It has always been a main road. The photograph above looks southeast, with the Park House Hotel in the background at the corner of Violet Avenue. Even in 1920, when significant amounts of snow were on the ground, horse-drawn transportation was still important. This sleigh was used for commercial purposes, to deliver goods most likely from the Howard A. James Hardware Store. The view below looks east, and the Episcopal church, built two years before, is at left in the distance. New commercial buildings were not located on the north side of Tulip Avenue, east of Violet Avenue, until the late 1920s. (Both, VFP.)

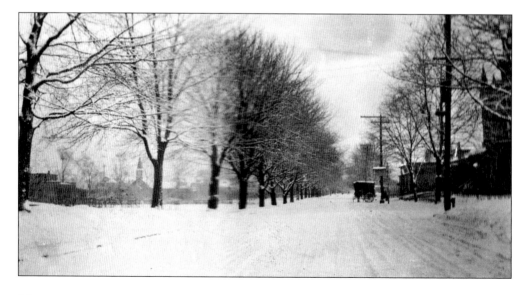

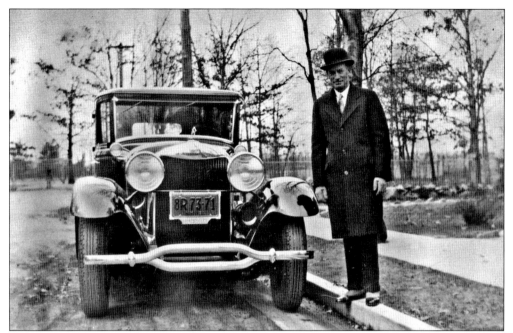

Walter G. Gosden is shown at the end of Mayfair Avenue in the west end of the village in front of his home with his new 1930 Lincoln sedan. The fence for Belmont Park can be seen in the background. Gosden was a contractor who specialized in concrete foundation and masonry work, and he built four homes in the west end for his family and children between 1925 and 1953. (W. Gosden.)

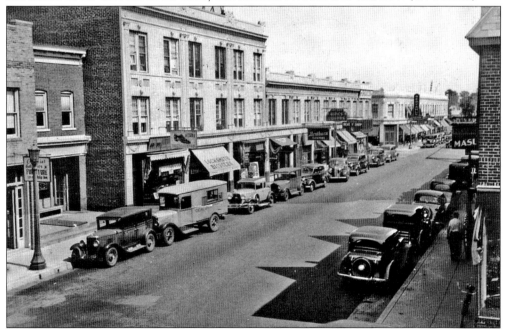

This view of Tulip Avenue was taken in 1936 from a second-floor apartment, located in the Ramee Pharmacy at 124 Tulip Avenue. The masonry buildings shown in the photograph were constructed in the 1929–1931 era and replaced all of the wood-frame structures and greenhouses that John Lewis Childs had built 45 years earlier. (W. Gosden.)

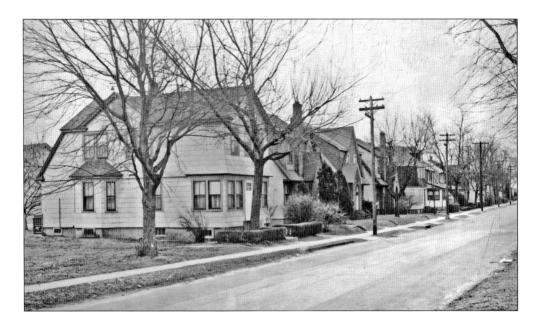

The era between the end of World War I and the early 1930s saw the development of vacant land at the northeast end of the village and the construction of a number of houses of assorted styles. Both these photographs were taken in 1938, with Sycamore Avenue pictured above and Beechurst Avenue shown below. For many decades, the land belonged to the Wicks family, whose property extended south below Jericho Turnpike and across the railroad tracks. By the time these images were taken, houses in the area had electricity, but all had cesspools, as public sewers were not installed until 1955. Most houses were still heated by coal as well. (Both, VFP.)

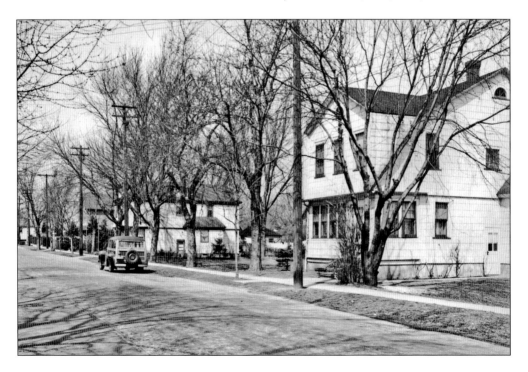

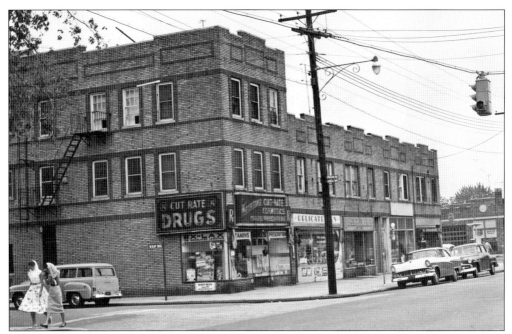

Gregory Mendelsohn's Drug Store was at the corner of Emerson Avenue and Jericho Turnpike. Former mayor Leslie Carpenter recalled that the store was closed on Sunday, but Mendelsohn would open for an emergency or illness. He and his wife, Rebecca, lived a few blocks away on Hawthorne Avenue and were a popular couple in the village. Rebecca Mendelsohn often sang the national anthem at public events. (VFP.)

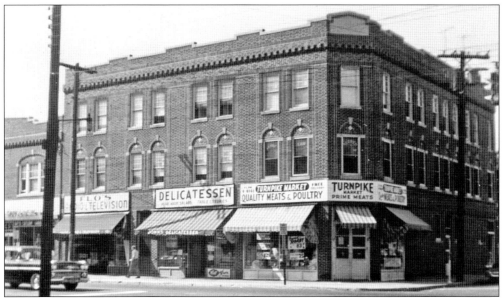

Dating from 1958, this view of the northwest corner of Jericho Turnpike and North Tyson Avenue shows the Turnpike Market. Floral Park had numerous butcher shops within it borders, as well as small local grocery stores. The proprietor of this market was also an artist and had numerous framed oil paintings around his store for sale. Many customers purchased these paintings while shopping there. (FPHS.)

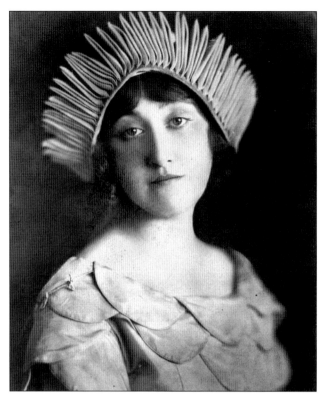

Jerome "Slim" Jackson (below, taken around 1935) and his wife, Alpha Hall (at left, taken around 1913), were well known on the vaudeville circuit, he in the team of Barber and Jackson and she in Norwood and Hall. As vaudeville performances declined with the introduction of talking motion pictures, the Jacksons moved to Floral Park and opened up a real estate office on Tulip Avenue in the 1930s. They were both well known in the village, and "Slim" Jackson gave volunteer performances at the American Legion. Both images date from their vaudeville days. She was 5 feet tall, and he was 6 foot, 6 inches tall, so as a couple, they were easy to recognize. (Both, Carson family.)

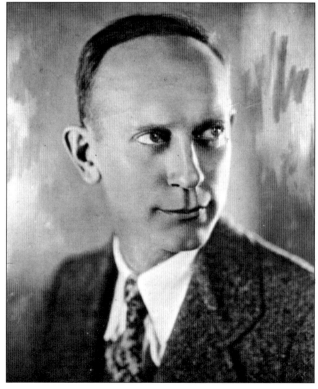

The Jerome Jackson real estate and insurance office was at 153 Tulip Avenue, and these images date from the early 1960s. The Jacksons were active in the business community, adding flair from their former years on the stage. Alpha Jackson kept an amazing flower garden behind their store and home, forever changing with the seasons. It was lush with color and maintained a variety of plants and flowers. The yard faced the village parking lot on Woodbine Court, and they were the only ones who kept up such a well-tended display among the concrete and macadam of this group of stores at the heart of the village. (Both, Carson family.)

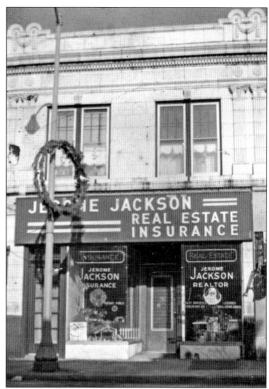

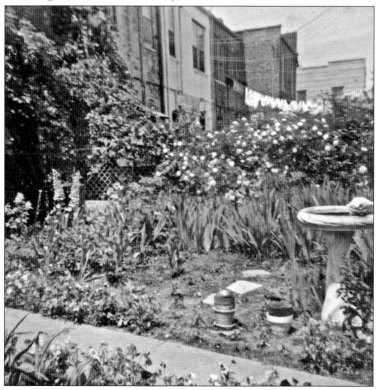

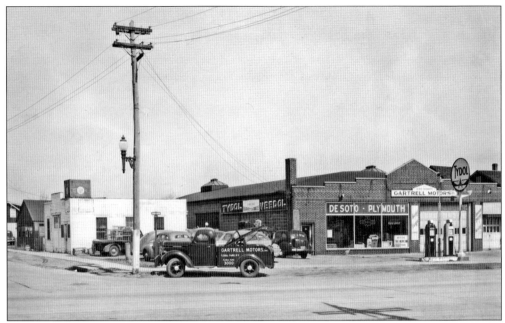

Gartell Motors was the local DeSoto-Plymouth car dealership in the 1930s and 1940s. The business was located at the east edge of the village on the north side of Jericho Turnpike. William Gartell was the proprietor and was active in the American Legion, becoming commander of the post in 1944. He and his wife, Anna, lived at 78 Holland Avenue, a few blocks west of his business. (VFP.)

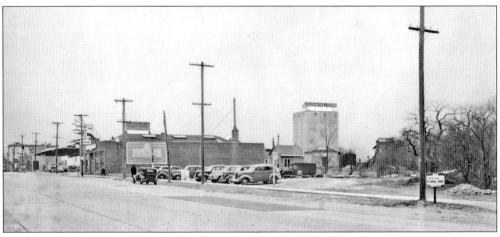

The area shown in this photograph, taken about 1938, is of Jericho Turnpike immediately east of the Creedmoor railroad bridge. It was built up as an industrial area in the 1930s. Although there were a few homes built on Garfield, Van Buren, and Van Siclen Avenues, most structures were commercial buildings. This image, looking south, shows the coal silos of the Vulcan and Colby-Julien fuel companies and a used-car lot. (VFP.)

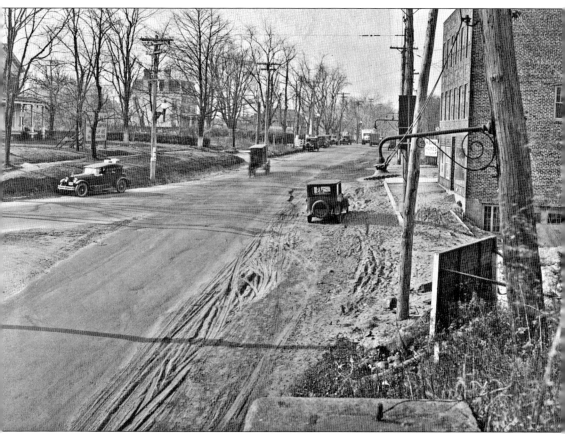

Dated November 23, 1927, this photograph shows Jericho Turnpike looking west, with Tulip Avenue coming in at left and Little Neck Parkway from the right, immediately past the masonry building. The brick building, which was never occupied, was torn down after a brief period. The area where the building was located, which is the north side of Jericho Turnpike, and the area beyond that is the border of Nassau and Queens Counties. The scene shown was still a rural setting with a paved two-lane road at the center and dirt shoulders. The second building from the left was the Floral Park Sanitarium, which functioned as a facility for decades, where numerous Floral Park and Bellerose residents were born or recuperated from illness. The image was taken from the iron railroad viaduct that passed over Jericho Turnpike, the main rail line that carried supplies to the New York State mental facility in Queens, just to the west. (VFP.)

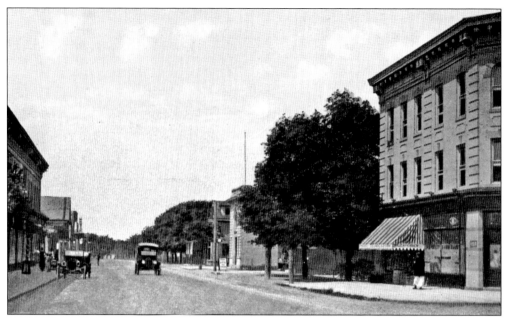

Both images show the south side of Jericho Turnpike at the corner of Garfield Avenue. The postcard image above dates from about 1920 and was published by Jacob Oshansky, who had a confectionery store across the street. The large three-story masonry building on the corner housed a delicatessen, as well as apartments on the two upper floors. The photograph below was taken in September 1959 and shows Herman's Tavern, located at that corner spot since the 1930s. Although there were many changes in proprietors over the decades, the tavern's name remained the same, closing only within the past few years. (Both, FPL.)

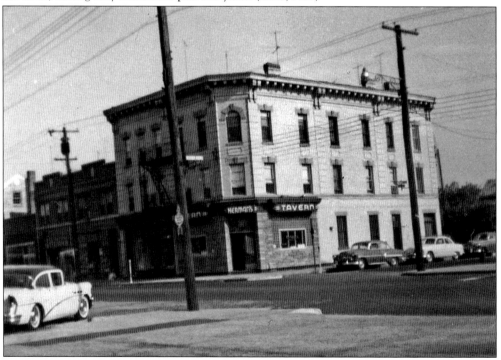

Six

NEW HORIZONS WITH TRADITIONAL VALUES

The postwar era saw Floral Park become a more full-service village, with its sanitation collection department, police department, fire department, and recreation department. The village playground was reworked and developed into a recreation center through the addition of a pool and a new multi-service building.

Several two-story garden apartment complexes were built on Tulip and Carnation Avenues, and the safe, family-oriented village was still only a 30-minute commute by train to downtown Brooklyn or Manhattan. This attracted many who worked in Manhattan to buy homes or rent apartments in the village.

The east end of the village, known as the Hillcrest area, had many Cape Cod–style houses, built there in the early 1950s. Local grocery stores, butcher shops, clothing stores, and pharmacies experienced competition arriving in the form of larger chain stores. Sewers were installed throughout the village in 1954 and 1955, and an additional high school was built at the southern edge of the village in 1957.

The most dramatic change took place from 1960 to 1962, when the train station was elevated to remove grade-level crossings, and the state widened Jericho Turnpike, demolishing almost all the buildings on the north side of that road. Decades passed before all of the land on that side of the road was rebuilt with new structures. Tradition did remain, with an annual Fireman's Day and tournament and going to the village playground to use the ball fields, tennis courts, swings, and seesaws.

A huge celebration was held in 1958 for the 50th anniversary of the village, for the 75th anniversary in 1983, and for the 100th anniversary in 2008. On these occasions, a number of residents were interviewed to capture their memories of the early days of life in the village.

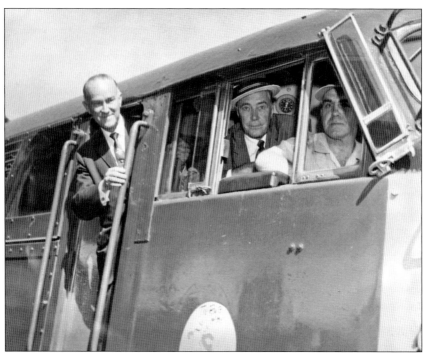

The transformation started in January 26, 1960, and after two and a half years, on June 28, 1962, the first train passed through the newly elevated Floral Park train station. Shown above, from left to right, are Floral Park mayor Leslie Carpenter, president of the Long Island Railroad Thomas Goodfellow, and engineer George Becker during the ceremonies. Becker not only worked as an engineer for the Long Island Railroad, but also resided in the village of Floral Park in the west end area. The photograph below shows the diesel engine passing through the wreath. For 30 years, the need to eliminate the ground-level grade crossings were campaigned for by the village. When plans were finalized, buildings and property were condemned for use, and the heart of the community was in a state of disruption. (Both, VFP.)

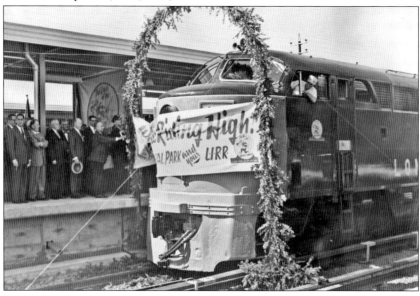

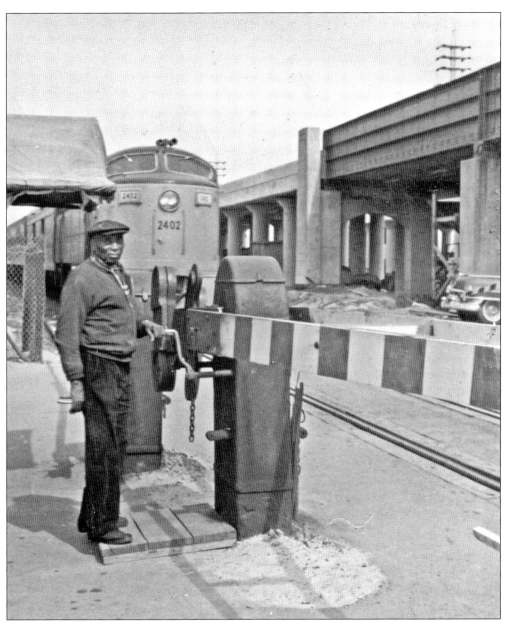

John H. Spriggs is shown on the job, serving as the gate man at the Tulip Avenue railroad crossing. This photograph dates from May 13, 1962, and as of that date, Spriggs had worked at that crossing to manually raise and lower the gates for 28 years. He was proficient at his job and was highly respected by all who met him. He was friendly and mailed out nearly 3,000 holiday and greeting cards each year to all who knew him. In the era before electrically equipped gate crossings, manual labor was used at every crossing throughout Long Island. The grade-level crossings created massive lines of traffic, especially when freight cars would pass by. In Floral Park, where two main lines joined two gate crossings only a block apart on Plainfield Avenue, if two trains were running fairly close together, it caused incredibly long lines of cars waiting to proceed. The Floral Park Lions Club honored John Spriggs in the mid-1950s for his kind and caring nature over the many decades. (VFP.)

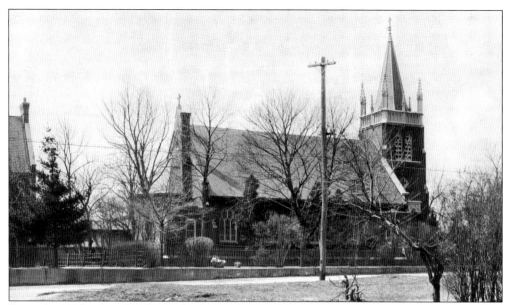

Since the 1800s, there has been a large population of families of Polish decent that have lived in the northeast section of Floral Park and in the areas to the east in New Hyde Park and Garden City Park. Many worked for John Lewis Childs in his flower fields and greenhouses, cultivating and packaging seeds and bulbs sold worldwide. A nearby Roman Catholic church where the Polish language was used to give Mass was of great need by this segment of the population. In 1902, St. Hedwig's Roman Catholic Church formed, and property on Jericho Turnpike between Linden and Depan Avenues was purchased. (Both, VFP.)

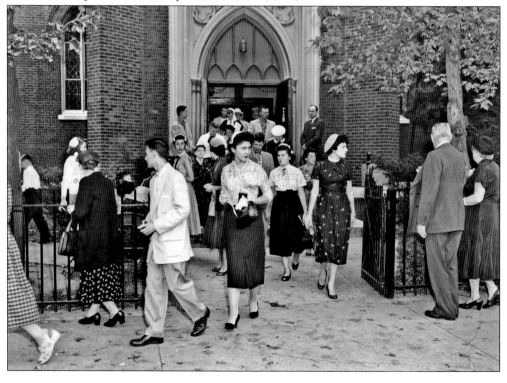

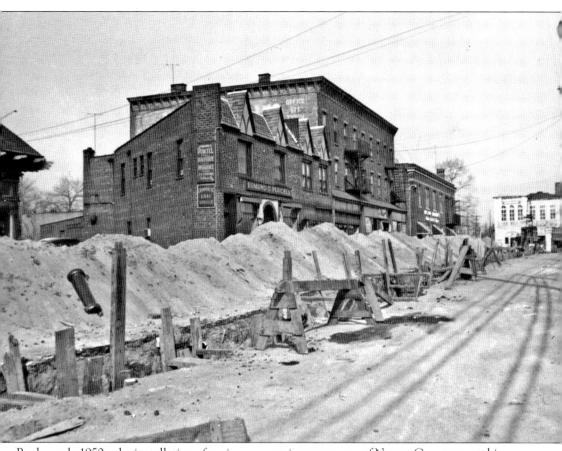

By the early 1950s, the installation of sanitary sewers in many areas of Nassau County was taking place. The Floral Park roadways were disrupted for months as this took place in 1955. This photograph shows the length of the Tyson Block torn up by the T&T Construction Company as work proceeded. The 1894 Tyson Building is at the center of the block, and just beyond that at the end of the block is Koenig's Restaurant, well known for its German-style food. Constructed in 1923 for the Knights of Columbus, the building served as a hall to hold their meetings and, at one time, was home to the Floral Park post office and library. During the poor economic times in the early 1930s, the building was sold and converted into a restaurant called the Tyson Club. Five years after this photograph was taken, the elevation of the train station once again disrupted the street for several years. (VFP.)

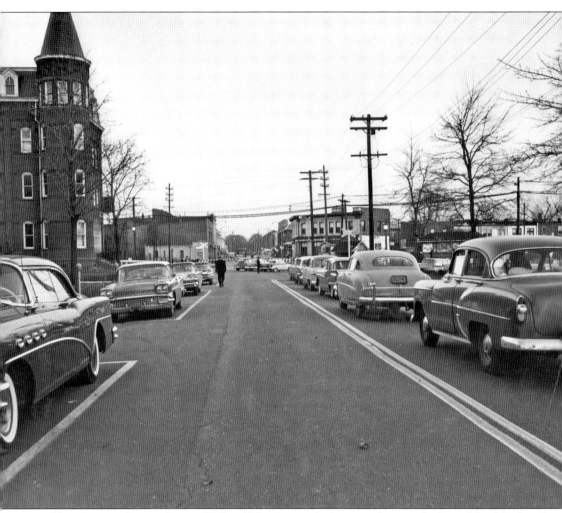

This photograph was taken in 1959 on Tulip Avenue looking southeast at the Long Island Railroad crossing. The crossing gates were hand operated, and long lines of traffic would develop that extended back nearly a quarter of a mile north and south on Tulip Avenue and nearby Carnation Avenue, just a block away. Freight trains, in particular, would cause long delays. At left is the former John Lewis Childs seed warehouse, with its tower and turret. At the center of the photograph is the Childs building constructed in 1909, which was home to a pharmacy operated by Clinton Ramee beginning in 1923. Traffic jams like this one led to the elevation of the train tracks and station, with work commencing a year after this photograph was taken. The pharmacy building was demolished, as were several other buildings that John Lewis Childs had built prior to 1900, when the work to elevate the rail began. (VFP.)

In the years prior to World War II, 150 Tulip Avenue was known to all as Dick's Confectionery Store. All varieties of ice cream flavors were served in sundaes, malts, and sodas. In the postwar years, the fare remained the same, but the name was changed to Schaefer's, as seen in the 1989 photograph at right. The neon and porcelain enamel sign was a familiar sight in the village for decades. (FPHS.)

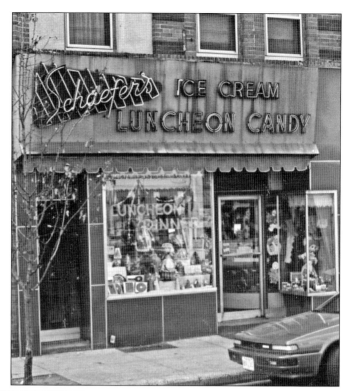

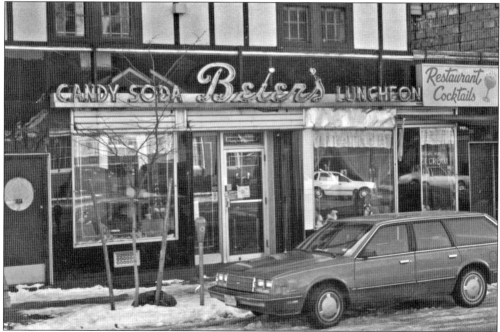

This photograph from 1989 shows Beier's luncheonette and confectionery store at 230 Jericho Turnpike. It was established before World War II as Zanetti's, named after the proprietors, Henry and Fernanda Zanetti. It served meals as well as fountain specialties. Known for their homemade chocolates, the Melosh family owned it in the postwar years. (FPHS.)

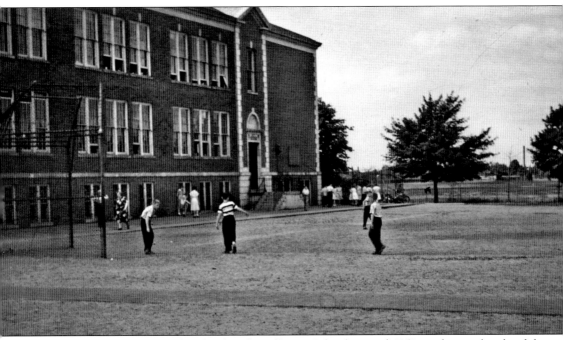

This photograph shows the Floral Park–Bellerose School around 1951 on the north side of the building looking west. Stickball was a favorite past time at recess, and the sand-filled lot was the perfect venue for this. The area was paved two decades later for use as a faculty parking lot, and an addition to the school was made at the same time to accommodate a new gymnasium and classrooms. The school was built in 1927–1929 and accommodates 1,000 children. It was named after the two communities that the elementary school district serves, and a pedestrian tunnel goes beneath the Long Island Railroad tracks on school property immediately to the right and just out of sight in this photograph. The large grassy area in the background was part of the Belmont Park racetrack, whose property borders the school, and was donated to the school district as a field for recreation for the children by the Westchester Racing Association, which owned Belmont Park at the time. (W. Gosden.)

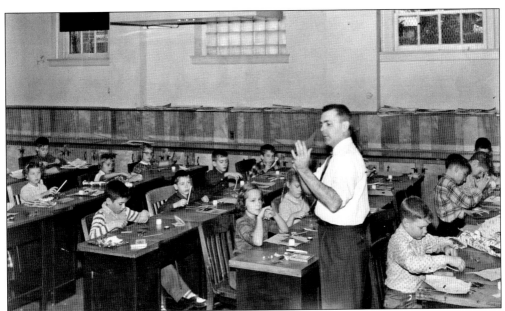

This photograph, dating from about 1959, was taken at the Floral Park–Bellerose School. It shows an art class in progress, with the art teacher, Clellan B. Chapman. The desks from when the school opened 30 years earlier were still in use. Chapman taught art from 1953 to 1982 and was an inspiration to thousands of students, including the author of this book. (FPHS.)

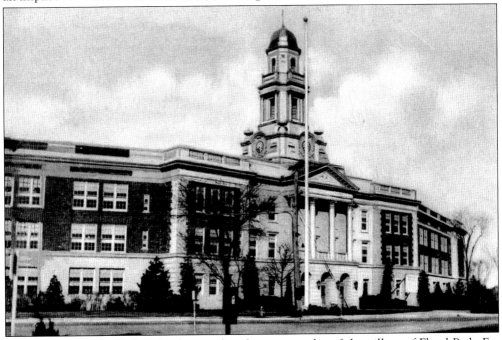

In 1930, Sewanhaka High School opened at the eastern edge of the village of Floral Park. For many years, vocational study programs were offered to students on a large scale, as well as academic classes. The student population at Sewanhaka High School outgrew the capacity of the building, and classes rotated to accommodate all the students until another, smaller high school was built nearby in Floral Park in 1957. (FPL.)

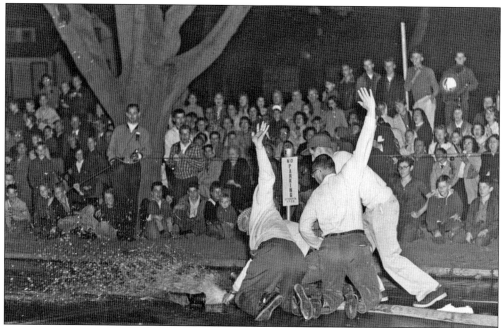

The annual Fireman's Day had been cause for celebration for most of the 20th century. It was held in various locations in the village, as space would allow, and the final tournaments were held on Floral Boulevard between Carnation and Verbena Avenues. During the year, the fire department teams from various areas would travel to the host town and participate in a parade, then in assorted competition events. Awards were presented for the fastest times in hose-hydrant connection, bucket brigade, hook and ladder, and more, all to a cheering crowd. These photographs show the 1958 event. Tournaments ceased in 1972 due to liability coverage and large crowds of spectators that became unmanageable. (Both, VFP.)

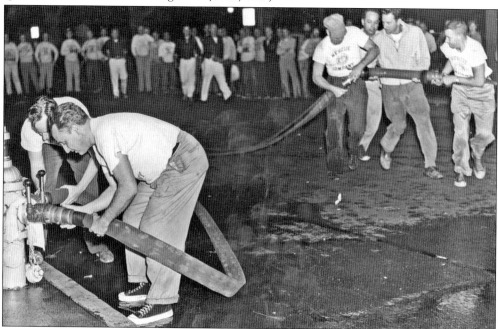

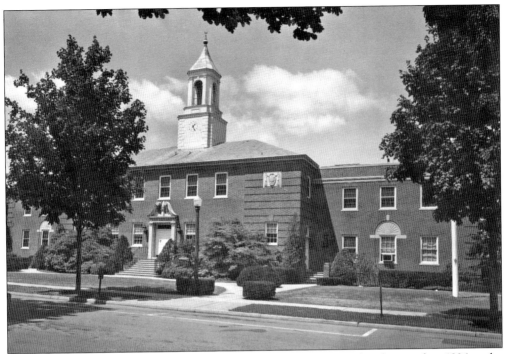

The Floral Park Village Hall, shown here in 1956, was built in 1935 and opened in 1936 at the north end of Floral Boulevard. It sits on land once owned by John Lewis Childs and was the scene of early baseball games. (VFP.)

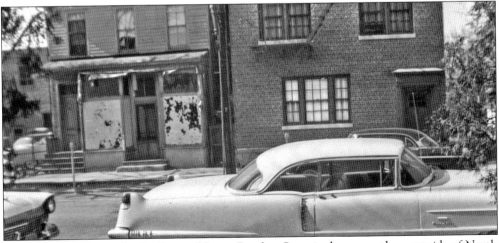

In this 1957 photograph, the Bernard Loew Butcher Store is shown on the west side of North Tyson Avenue. In 1904, Loew had his shop in the Tyson Block facing the railroad tracks, and shortly afterward, he moved to the store shown here. He was elected as a trustee of the village in 1925 and served in that capacity until his death in 1927. (VFP.)

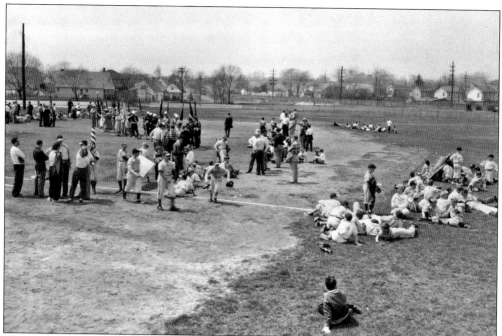

The Floral Park Bombers sports group formed in the 1930s to keep the ball season going longer. It went from an informal group in 1936 to an incorporated organization in 1946. The softball team participated in several leagues and was the Nassau County basketball champion in the post–World War II era. In 1953, Little League teams were organized, with games played at the Floral Park Village Playground on Stewart Street. This playground area is located at the border of New Hyde Park between the Long Island Railroad Hempstead and Mineola branch lines. These photographs show the playground ball fields in the early 1950s, with the old grandstand that was replaced around 1956. (Both, VFP.)

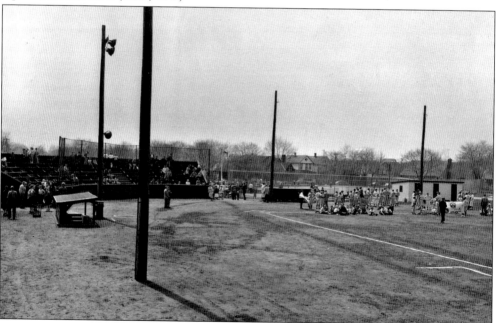

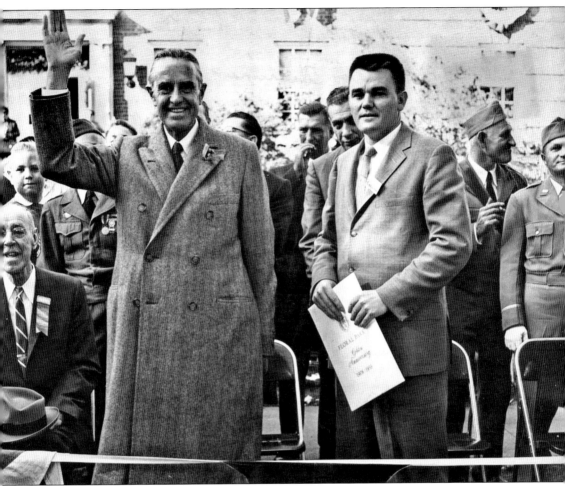

The 50th anniversary of the Village of Floral Park was celebrated with a huge parade in 1958. New York State governor W. Averall Harriman attended the festivities and is shown in this photograph, taken in front of Floral Park Village Hall. Pictured from left to right are (seated) former mayor Walter Lawrence (1951–1955), Governor Harriman, and John F. English, the aide to the governor, standing next to him holding the Golden Anniversary program. Harriman was in familiar territory, as he frequently visited Belmont Park before and after he was governor. He had a great interest in thoroughbred racing and owned a stable of horses. Harriman was the 48th governor of the State of New York and served one term in office, from January 1955 to December 1958. He was a Democrat that, through his friendship with Pres. Harry Truman, was named ambassador to the Soviet Union in 1945 and then to Great Britain in 1946. (VFP.)

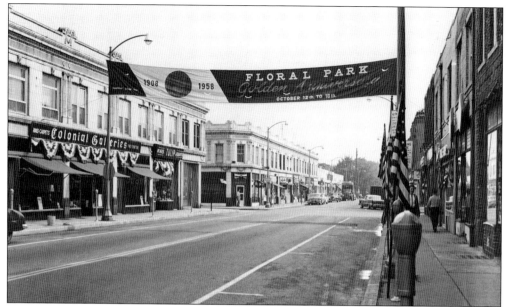

The Golden Anniversary of the Village of Floral Park was celebrated from October 12–18, 1958, after years of planning. The image above shows Tulip Avenue looking southeast toward Plainfield Avenue, with the buildings decorated for the festivities. The photograph below shows Miss Golden Anniversary, Mary Elizabeth Farrell, on a float during the anniversary parade on October 18. At the time this photograph was taken, the parade had just turned onto Floral Boulevard and was about to pass the reviewing stand in front of the village hall. The name "Flowerland" on the float harks back to the era prior to 1900, when Childs had his acres of flowers that could be seen by the railroad train passengers. (Both, VFP.)

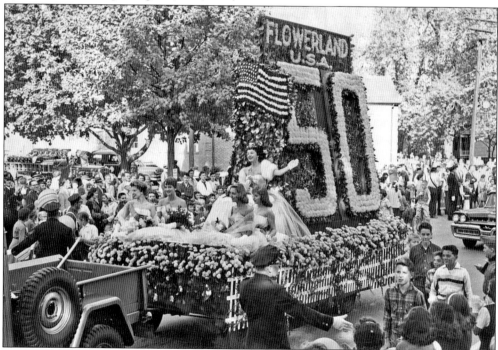

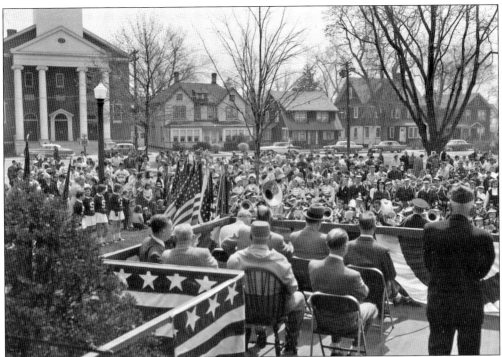

In April 1956, "I Am An American Day" was celebrated and coincided with the opening of Little League, Babe Ruth, and Connie Mack leagues' baseball season. This image shows the speaker's stand, erected on the front lawn of the village hall on Floral Boulevard. The view is southeast with the Methodist church and shows houses on Verbena Avenue in the background. (VFP.)

Charles Jurgens opened his Fancy Groceries store at 134 Tulip Avenue in 1922. Located on the south side of the street, his neighbors to the east were a bakery and Drew's Butcher Shop. Within 70 feet, a resident could get all of their food shopping done. Henry Jurgens, shown at right, followed in his father's business, but competition from chain food stores forced Jurgens Grocery Store to close when he retired in 1970. (VFP.)

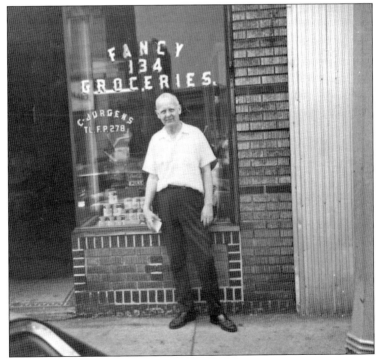

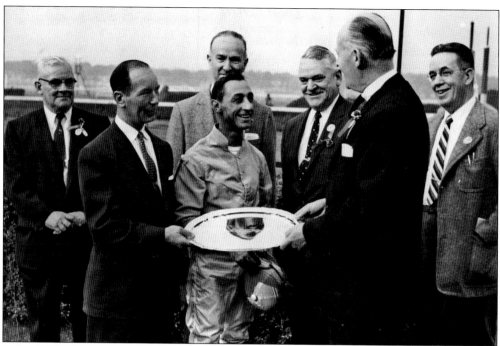

Jockey Eddie Arcaro was a legend in his own time as a successful jockey that rode many thoroughbred racehorses to victory. The above photograph shows the ceremony at Belmont Park after the Floral Park Anniversary race in 1958. Pictured from left to right are (first row) unidentified, jockey Eddie Arcaro (who won the race), and Mayor William Lewis; (second row) village clerk Charles Hartman and village trustees Leslie Carpenter, Frank Lopez, and John McConville. In the photograph below is the Arcaro and Dan's Saddlery, which was located on Jericho Turnpike for many years. When this view was taken in 1959, the business had just vacated when news of the building's eminent destruction was announced by the state, which would widen the road the next year. (VFP and FPHS.)

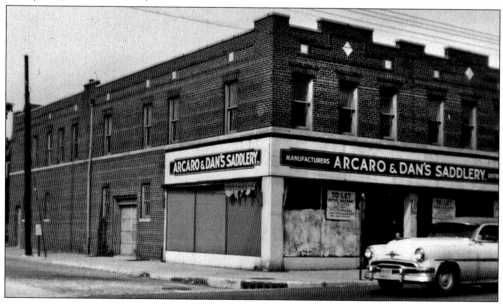

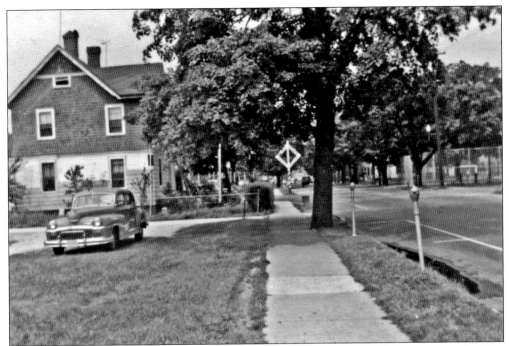

This 1958 photograph shows the house built by George Tyson around 1895. It was just south of the railroad crossing of the Creedmoor Spur. The Joel Hayden family occupied the house on South Tyson Avenue for several years, followed by Adoph Jaenicke, who was supervising horticulturist for John Lewis Childs, in 1900. The Floral Park School was located to the north, diagonally across the street. (VFP.)

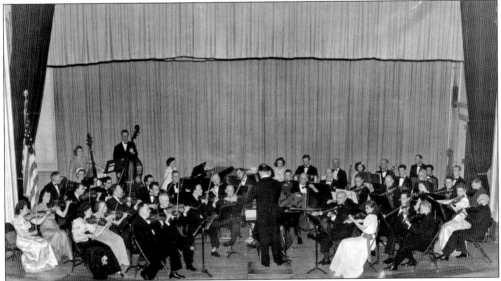

Organized in 1942 for morale building purposes, the Floral Park Citizen's Defense Corps Orchestra existed for approximately a decade. This photograph was taken on May 11, 1945, as they performed at the Floral Park–Bellerose School. Edmund D. Purcell was the president of the organization and would become village historian from 1955 to 1960. George Weigel was the conductor of the orchestra, and William Fenno was assistant conductor. (VFP.)

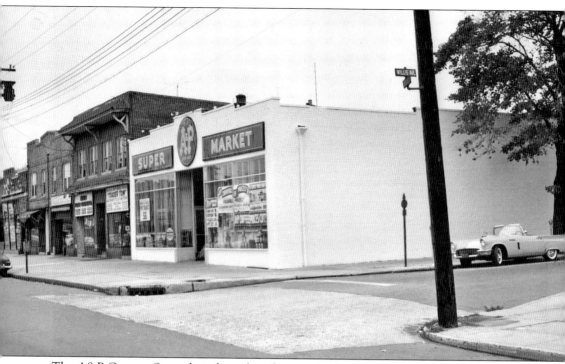

The A&P Grocery Store chain has a long history in Floral Park, with the first stores appearing prior to World War II on Verbena and Covert Avenues. The Great Atlantic and Pacific Tea Company was a family-owned business and had the first larger grocery stores in Floral Park, with store locations at the center and eastern border of the village. This photograph was taken in 1957 and shows a thriving A&P supermarket on Jericho Turnpike at Willis Avenue. The "supermarket" had just been introduced in the late 1950s, and the store shown above was the first of its kind in the area. All of the stores along Jericho Turnpike in 1960 were torn down with the widening of the road by the state except for this one. St. Hedwig's Catholic Church is across the street, and they negotiated to purchase the building and renovated it, adding a second floor to convert it into a parish hall. (VFP.)

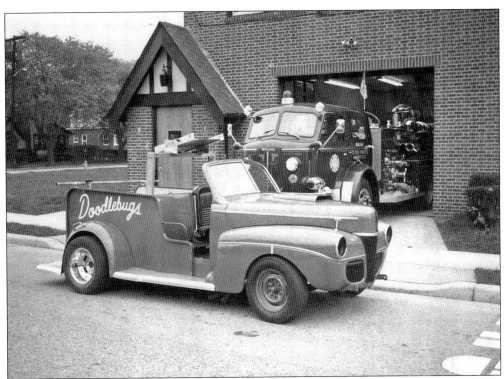

Floral Park's fire department tournament team was named the Doodlebugs. There was active competition between town fire departments, and special trucks were specifically built by volunteers in the department for the tournaments. This photograph, dating from 1972, is in front of the Active Company Firehouse on Atlantic Avenue, with their 1957 American LaFrance pumper in the background and the tournament truck out front. (William Green.)

Mayor George Farrell (right) congratulates fire department chief Lawrence McCabe upon the unveiling of the fireman's memorial monument on the front lawn of the library on August 1, 1965. The bell on the monument was the school bell for the Floral Park School when it opened in 1895. When the original school building was torn down in 1958, the bell was saved and given to the fire department. (VFP.)

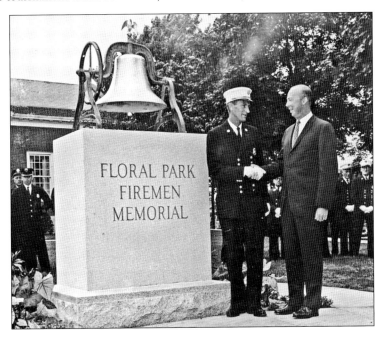

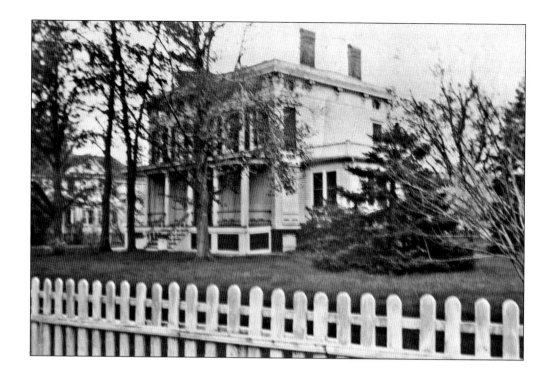

The Covert family, early property owners and settlers in the area at the east end of the village, built three large houses on the north side of Light Horse Road, and their property ran north for nearly 1 mile beyond the Long Island Railroad tracks. The first house was at Covert Avenue, named for the family who donated the property to the county for the road. This grand home, built in the mid-1800s, can be seen in the photograph above, taken in the early 1950s. All three Covert houses were similar in style and had huge barns in back of their deep property. In the mid-1950s, the original house and contents were auctioned off, and the house was demolished. Deemed as commercial property, the Food Fair store in the photograph below was built in its place. (Both, VFP.)

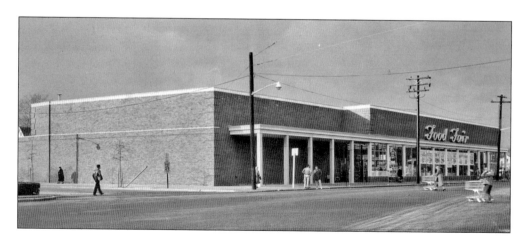

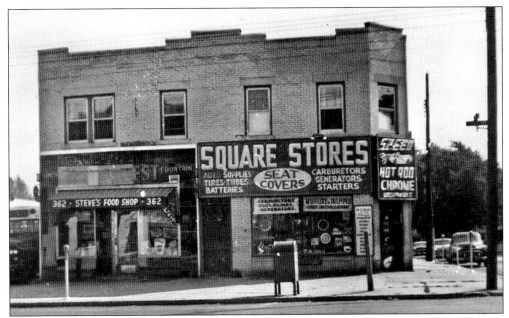

The Square Speed Shop on Jericho Turnpike, adjacent to the property of St. Hedwig's church, was a haven and "heaven" for hot-rodders. The store offered a huge selection of mechanical parts and machine shop service to hop up a car. The sign above the door proclaimed, "Speed: Hot Rod Chrome Equipment." What the shop did not have it could get in a short period of time. This photograph dates from 1959. (FPHS.)

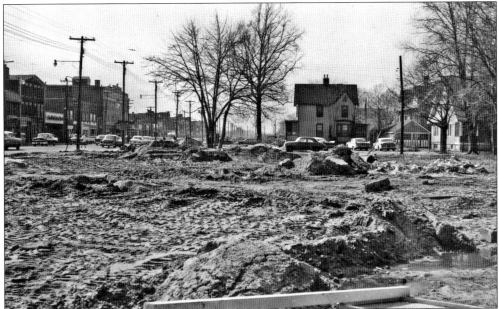

The state highway improvement project in 1960–1961 demolished 64 buildings along the north side of Jericho Turnpike, from the Queens-Nassau County line east. Demolition started in May 1960, and by December 1961, Jericho Turnpike was widened and completely resurfaced. The total distance was 2.35 miles. This photograph is from February 1961 and is looking west from Emerson Avenue. The home of Bessie Keithley remains standing at center. (FPHS.)

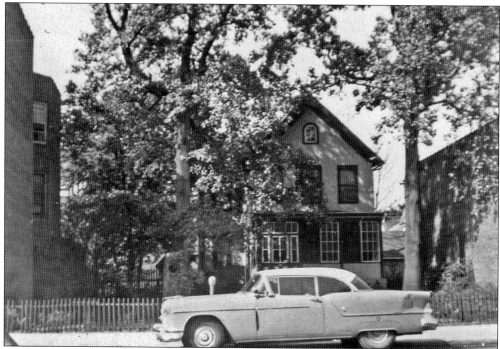

When this photograph was taken in 1959, this house, at 243 Jericho Turnpike, was the last private dwelling between Tyson and Emerson Avenues. It was built prior to 1900 and was part of George Tyson's property. The Keithley family had owned the property since the World War I era. (FPHS.)

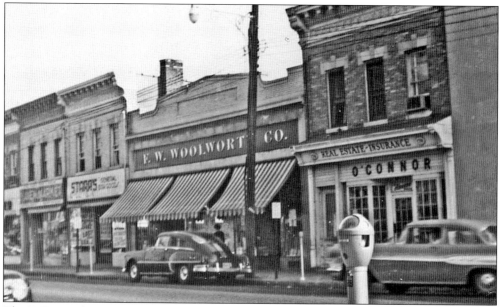

The F. W. Woolworth Company store was a fixture in the community for 50 years. By the time this photograph was taken in September of 1959, thousands of moms, with kids in hand, had crossed the threshold of the store. They explored the counters topped with glass-divided bins to seek out household supplies at this 5 and 10¢ store. (FPHS.)